Francis Chinedu Okenwa

Your Place in Christ

Francis Chinedu Okenwa

Your Place in Christ

...understanding your privileges in Christ

Blessed Hope Publishing

Imprint

Cover image: www.ingimage.com

Publisher:
Blessed Hope Publishing
is a trademark of
International Book Market Service Ltd., member of OmniScriptum Publishing Group
17 Meldrum Street, Beau Bassin 71504, Mauritius
Printed at: see last page
ISBN: 978-613-7-97448-3

YOUR PLACE
IN
CHRIST

OKENWA FRANCIS CHINEDU

CONTENT

DEDICATION

To the Almighty God who has been the greatest investor in knowledge throughout the ages. Who also has inspired me to put this work together

To every believer that has been in search of the realities of Christ in this generation where truth has become obscure and falsehood has taken over the church.

To all that has taught me in the cause of putting together this work over the past eight years, I dedicate this to you also for all your labor of love.

INTRODUCTION

'' And the Lord God formed man of the dust of the ground and breathe into his nostrils the breath of life; and man became a living soul. And the Lord God planted a garden eastward in Eden and there He put the man whom He had formed'' Gen. 2:7-8.

From the first time I heard the story of creation, I have always wondered what happened to the garden God planted and gave man to take care of in the beginning and whenever I had opportunities, I always tried to ask people who I believe are deep in the knowledge of the word of God and yet none of them was able to give an answer that sufficed. Some said the garden is in an undiscoverable portion of the earth where no scientific compass can detect. Others said because of the angel with a flaming sword that was placed at the entrance of the garden, humans can't find it, but do you really think Eden is on the earth? As we are about to begin this journey to discovering our place in Christ, understanding of this matter is very important. Let's begin by taking another look at the text. The bible did not tell us that Eden is on earth, but one thing of certain is that Eden is a place.

''And the Lord planted a garden eastward in Eden, and there He put the man whom He had formed''.

Eden is a place; it is a realm of operation. It is not a location on the surface of the earth, Eden is a realm in the spirit where God placed the man He had formed. From the creation of man, man was never meant to operate from the realm of the earth like the other beasts of the air, sea and the land do. God put man on the earth operating from a realm above the earth. Eden means delight or pleasure; it was the realm of operation of the first man from where he will bring pleasure to God and give him delight. During the time humankind operated from Eden, he completely brought pleasure to God in his actions and decisions, infact man was in harmony with the spirit of God and spoke and did the mind of God consistently.

Thou art worthy, O Lord, to receive glory and honour and power: for thou hast created all things, and for thy pleasure they are and were created. Rev 4:11

In this realm, man could see and learn from the creativity of God as he continues in the work of creation. The moment man was sent out from operating from Eden to operate in the realm of earth, the first murder in scripture happened. The two sons of Adam who he gave birth to in his fallen image could no longer understand the perfect will of God so while they went to make an offering to God, Abel offered an acceptable sacrifice while Cain was rejected. From the realm of earth man was left to guess the heart of God and no longer had such perfect understanding of the desires of the Father hence man could no longer bring God pleasure. Infact the situation on the earth realm went so bad to the point that every thought of man's heart was displeasing to God continually. All these happened when man left his realm of operation to operate from the earthly dimension even till today.

Eden was the realm of the untested man, the unproved man that God made, where God will prove him. This was the reason why the Lord God caused all manners of beautiful trees to grow from the ground, the tree of life and the tree of the knowledge of good and evil. There were three categories of trees in Eden, which the Lord God wanted the man to make a choice out of, the trees that were pleasant to the sight and good for food, the tree of life and tree of knowledge of good and evil. And the Lord God told man to choose freely out of these trees with a command not to choose the tree of the knowledge of good and evil. Eden is a realm where God will prove the man He had formed. The choice was supposed to be between the trees that are pleasant to sight and good for food (walking by sight or living like the beasts of the earth) and the tree of life (living the God kind of life). This choice was going to determine the next dimension of operation of man and how his relationship with God will become. The realm of Eden was also a realm where it was easy for man to hear God and speak to him also. This was perfectly portrayed when the Lord God formed all the beasts of the earth and brought them to the man, it was easy for the man to know what God would have called them and so he did and that became the name for such beasts. Even that exercise was brought about by God's desire to make a help meet for the man. The man could have chosen any of the beasts for mate, but because he was connected to the mind of God, he could only call them names but did not take any as a mate. And when the Lord God took a rib from the man after he fell asleep and formed a woman, He also brought it to the man who from his spirit knew it was one that looks like himself, the bone of his bone and he called her woman. It is important to say that there was no mirror those days, Adam had never seen how he looked to think the woman looked like him hence his response was not a response due to appearance, but it was a result of the connection in the spirit. While in Eden Adam was able to operate like God from the dimension of a higher wisdom than the wisdom of earth. So in Eden, recognizing the voice of God was not a problem for the man and he always walked in perfect harmony with the Spirit of God. Eden is a spiritual realm that the first man operated from while yet on the earth. It was going to be the beginning of the dimensions of man's operation with God had it not been for its sudden termination as a result of the devil's deceptive plan.

THE RIVER OF EDEN

''And a river went out of Eden to water the garden, and from thence it was parted and became four heads''Gen. 2:10

The bible also brings to light a very important feature of the dimension called Eden – the river. It said a river went out of Eden to water the garden. This river represents the Spirit of God. Even before man could step into his assignment, the Spirit of God went ahead of him, to prepare the place, to water the garden else; there is absolutely nothing the man can do. The assignment God had for man was to till the Garden so that the trees can grow, but the Spirit of God will go ahead of the man to prepare the ground to respond to the man. No matter how hard you think God's assignment for your life is, I want you to know that the Holy Spirit has already gone ahead of you to cause things to fall in place if only you will act. Just like a river went out of Eden to wet the ground for man's easy tilling, so also the Spirit of God has gone ahead of you to make everything answer to you when you call.

However, the river didn't just water the garden alone, it went further and parted into four heads to supply water also to the earth. It became four rivers on earth which were called Pishon, which compasses the land of Havilah, the land where Ishmael dwells, the second river was called Gihon that compasses the land of Ethiopia, the third, Hiddekel and the last is Euphrates.

The river of Eden went beyond the realm of Eden and manifested also in the realm of the physical for man's benefit. When the Lord walked the earth he taught his disciples that when we receive the Holy Spirit as the water that the Holy Spirit becomes a river of living water flowing out of our belly. The river of God (Holy Spirit) is not stagnant water, but a flowing river and just same way the river of Eden flowed and formed other rivers on earth that we can see and know today, the Holy Spirit in us must be seen and known by people around us if he indeed dwells in us. Also these rivers had significant impact on the lands where they flowed so also the presence of the Spirit of God in us must have a significant impact both on us and our environment.

THE FALL OF MAN

In the midst of all this gory in Eden, there was a problem, the devil could also operate in this dimension. This was the major problem with Eden, the devil being able to operate in this dimension. No wonder when he was cast out of heaven and there was no place for him, he came to Eden and deceived man in order to put enmity between God and man. Despite the Holy Spirit that has been in the garden walking and teaching man how to tend it, yet man was swayed to yield to the voice of the serpent. After the deception of the devil, the woman began to see the tree of knowledge of good and evil in same category as the trees that were pleasant to the eye and good for food. If she had been looking for trees that were good for food and pleasant to the eyes, they were in the garden and the tree of the knowledge of good and evil was not one of them. It is only when a man has been taken by deception that he begins to mistake to see differently from the reality. There were trees that are pleasant to the eyes and good for food, then one tree of life and one tree of knowledge of good and evil. How come they could not look among the pleasant trees, if they were looking for trees good for food? They didn't need to look far; God had already declared some trees as good for food and pleasant to the eyes. It was just a question of deception of the devil and man fell for it. Now even after their eyes were open, they were still able to hear the voice of God because they were still in the realm called Eden. But so that man will not also take of the tree of life and eat and live forever in his state, God sent man out of the realm of Eden, to till the ground from where he was formed. The fall of man was man's disconnection from the realm above earth where God created him to live and operate from to living in the realm of earth and operating like the other beast of earth. This was never God's plan for man; it was only a result of man's rebellion. From creation, God had destined man to operate from realms above the earth, operating beyond the limitations of earth and continuing the work God called us to do from the beginning. This is the reason why man came so low to living the life of sin and every imaginations of man's heart was evil and wicked. Also from the realm of earth, man is no longer in harmony with the mind of God to know what God wants him to do per time. Man's desire was shifted from pleasing God which is the reason why humankind was created in the first place to seeking to please self.. Man became totally cut off from God and so more opened to the voice of the devil, because if you cannot listen to the voice of God, you will definitely listen to the voice of the devil. But God had another plan, the devil was not aware of, a better plan than the first would have ever been. This was the salvation of mankind through Jesus.

CHAPTER 1

THE NEW CREATION

''Therefore if any man be in Christ, he is a new creature; old things are passed away; behold , all things are become new'' 2Cor. 5:17.

The story of the fall of man would have been very painful had it not been that God also prepared another story, a better story than the former. It is the story of the creation and exaltation of man. This is the story of the new creation. The devil thought he had given man the devastating blow that will destabilize him forever, but he didn't know that God actually had another plan. Many times, the events of life turn the glorious story of your life upside down, just at the peak of your story and it feels like the world has come to an end, you cannot find another reason to carry on, you wish yourself death, I want you to know that at that same situation God has another plan. God has never been handicapped by the misfortunes that come on the part of man's destiny. He always has a way of accounting them for your benefit. In the garden of Eden, after man disobeyed God and made the worst choice of his life, God drove the man out of the garden so that he does not complicate his case, and from that moment, God started making His move for the redemption of man, in fact, the lamb of God, the bible said was slained before the foundation of the earth. So it wasn't surprising to God, because He already took that to record. Pastor Tunde Bakare will always say *'' the moment the events of your life becomes a surprise to God, then He ceases to be God''*. One of the things that make God, God which you and I must never forget is that He is all knowing and has the ability to see the end from the beginning. when the scriptures says God knows the end from the beginning, it is not talking about the way you have an idea of the outcome of something, neither is it talking about anticipating an end or outcome from the beginning, that is obtainable with man, but God knows the details of your end from the beginning, the full knowledge of everything that will happen in that process from the very beginning to the very end. A song writer put it this way – to you my future is a memory, because you are already there. So God is fully aware of all those hitches you are just noticing now. A little of this can be explained with the example of our Lord Jesus. He chose 12 disciples for himself, from the very first day, he knew the one who would betray him, how he will betray him even where and when it was going to happen. One thing that baffles me is how Christ could have all these details about Judas, his purpose, his personality and yet be so calm and related with the man very normal even to the point of making him the treasurer off the ministry.

To the natural man, once he has an idea of a possible harm you will cause him, even if he cannot remove you so you do not bring the harm, he will relate very unfriendly with you. This is exactly the reason God will not tell you about those misfortunes or pains/disappointments that are set to come your way, because the knowledge of it will end up weighing you down a thousand times before it manifest. So God knew about the serpent's deception, that was why He discouraged man from eating the tree of knowledge of good and evil by commanding them not to eat it. God always knew about the fall of man and so He made a way back to him for man. The Lamb of God was slain before the foundation of the earth, but was revealed in these last days for our redemption. Jesus came as the last Adam to come and rewrite the story of the first Adam.

''For as by one man's disobedience many were made sinners, so by the obedience of one shall many be made righteous'' Rom.5: 19

Adam sinned and it was imputed to all mankind; this is because all mankind were born from Adam, The bible said God created man in His image after His likeness but Adam begets children in his own likeness after his image. Gen.5:3. So the transgression of the first man was transferred to all men so all were sinners. Sin was imputed to all mankind even those who had not sinned after the similitude of Adam's transgression. This was the state of the first Adam and his descendants. But even in this mess, God had a plan. A plan to recreate mankind by sending another man Jesus Christ. It was important that Christ would come in the form of man, if he must fully pay the redemption price for their salvation. But much more, for Christ to pay for the sins of men, he must not be a partaker of the same sin. Many were made sinners not because they sinned like Adam but because they were born in the likeness of Adam and in his image. This is the reason for the miraculous conception of the messiah – a virgin shall be with child. So there was no contribution of man in the conception of the Lord. This is why Christ can be called the last Adam. By the disobedience of the first Adam, all became sinners. So the last Adam came and fulfilled God's requirement, so that by his obedience many shall be made righteous. The purpose for Christ's coming was not to die for you and me, but to recreate a new breed, the new creation. The death of Christ was a price to pay in order to achieve the purpose. And now that Christ has died and is risen, he paid the price for the new man; and the door was now open for as many that want to enter into this new life. The door to enter to this new life is Christ through the process of being born again. The concept of born again is our Lord Jesus' idea, not the Pentecostal chanting, it is real, Christ spoke to the teacher of the Hebrews; except a man be born again, he cannot see the kingdom of God. This is because just like all men are born in the likeness of Adam and in his own image, making them sinners so as many that will be born again in the likeness of the last Adam, after his own image are declared righteous. So except a man is born again, he retains the image and likeness of Adam that he was born with and as Adam has to be disconnected from Eden and sent to operate in the realms of earth, so will such persons live an earthly limited life. A life of ''seeing is believing'' instead of a superior life of ''believing is seeing''. Operating in the realm of earth brings a distortion to man's function. No wonder human beings now sleep with animals, because they are now set on the same realm with these beasts. But in the beginning it was not so. Even when Adam was given an opportunity to find a companion among the beasts of the earth, he couldn't find any, even dog was there, but could not be qualified as a companion for man because none of them operated from Eden. Today it is different, animals have become close companions of human being than fellow humans. This is because man now operates in the same realm as these animals. But Christ came to recreate mankind, to birth a new creation that no longer operates in the realm of earth but in a realm far above earth.

''who hath delivered us from the power of darkness and hath translated us into the kingdom of his dear son'' Gal. 1:13.

At the point of new birth, i.e. being born again, a remarkable event occurs. Man became translated from operating from the realm of earth to another realm - The realms of the kingdom of Christ. This is the place called ''in Christ Jesus''. This is the realm of operation of the recreated man. The descendants of the last Adam operates from this realm. Anybody that is found in this realm, the scriptures refer to as the new creation. You become new specie different from the specie called man of earth.

Your spirit man comes back to life, so that even though you walk on the earth, you operate from a realm far above the realm of earth. This is a place to be. One good thing about this place called – in Christ Jesus is that it is open to any man. It is not an opening for Jews alone or Greeks, it is for any man. So far as you are a man born in the likeness of the first Adam and after his image, you qualify for this translation. However it is not everyman that has been translated to this place- Christ Jesus. In Adam, you don't have a choice, you are just born and you carry the sin of Adam with you but you must choose whether or not you want to be born again – which is your entry point to this new realm – Christ Jesus. The way to enter is just as the scripture puts it

''if you confess with your mouth, the Lord Jesus and believe in thine heart, that God raised him from the dead, so shall you be saved'' Rom 10:9.

It is as simple as this, it is a question of the heart, a question of choice. It is no longer for you to blame Adam, you have become your own Adam, and the choices of God are before you, it is up to you to choose. As for God, he will always say – choose life so that you will live thereby. But the choice is up to you now.

WHAT HAPPENS IN CHRIST JESUS?

''And all things are of God, who hath reconciled us to himself by Jesus Christ and given us to us the ministry of reconciliation, to wit that God was in Christ, reconciling the world unto Himself, not imputing their trespasses unto them; and hath committed unto us the word of reconciliation'' 2Cor 5:18-19.

One significant thing about this place – in Christ Jesus is God's presence in it. It is not like the Garden of Eden where God comes down to fellowship with man in the cool of the day, here God is already there waiting for you. It is the new creation going up to meet with God in Christ Jesus. God in Christ is not there to condemn and declare judgment like He did when He showed up in Eden and man had made the wrong choice. In Christ, God was and is there reconciling the world unto Himself, not imputing their trespasses unto them. This is glorious. When God came to Eden He declared judgment on man's choice and his sins were imputed to him and he became responsible for the consequences that followed. But in Christ, God was reconciling the world unto Himself, taking us back instead of casting us out by wiping out every ordinance and writing of accusation that was against us. God was in Christ, reconciling the world to Himself. The word ''world'' as used here means mankind, the human race. God was reconciling the human race to Himself no longer imputing their trespass against them. The only place to be friend again with God is only in Christ, for there God ended the enmity between Himself and man and started afresh walk. This is one important event that occurs at new birth, once a man has been translated to this place – in Christ Jesus, he becomes reconciled to God. Every event of his past becomes wiped away with the precious blood of Christ and much more; there is a recreation of His spirit man – in the image and after the likeness of the last Adam Christ Jesus. You acquire the seed – the nature and likeness of Christ, just like you acquired that of the first Adam at natural birth.

''nevertheless death reigned from Adam to Moses, even over them that had not sinned after the similitude of Adam's transgression, who is the figure of him that was to come'' Rom 5:14.

When Adam sinned, and the sin of Adam automatically came upon every one that is a seed of Adam even when they had not disobeyed God like Adam did. The sins of Adam became inherent for mankind, so that none was righteous. This, the bible said was a figure of him that was to come. so that just as Adam's sin was reckoned to all men just because all were born in his likeness after his image, so also the righteousness of Christ is accounted to all who come to this place – in Christ Jesus, through the door of new birth. You become the righteousness of God not just because of anything you have done, or anything you are doing or anything you will ever do, it is because of the nature of whom you are born.

You are now born with the likeness and image of Christ, so righteousness is imputed to you because of Jesus Christ. So if any man is in Christ, he can never be a sinner, because the seed of Christ is in him. This is what John wanted to tell the church when he wrote;

''whosoever is born of God doth not commit sin; for his seed remaineth in him, and he cannot sin because he is born of God'' I John 3:9

There is no sin in Christ; because we have received the righteousness of God through Jesus Christ... sin becomes an alien to the new creature, righteousness becomes and must become our emphasis not sin, because we have been delivered from it. Man was a slave of sin not because he loved sin, it is not convenient to be a sinner, but man was made a sinner because he was born with the nature of sin from Adam, so man cannot help but sin. Now the new creature is born with the nature of righteousness and I can tell you it is not easy to live righteous especially with the perversity in our world today, but this is our nature, we cannot deny it. Our manifestation of this nature of righteousness must begin with us understanding that we have received the nature of righteousness and accept God's declaration over our lives – the righteousness of God in Christ. Then we must make conscious effort to be who God has said we are. We must let the righteousness of God shine forth through us in this world. Though in the bid to be who God has declared us to be, we may go contrary to His word, it is not the same as sin, it is now called trespass i.e. stepping beyond your boundary or right or territory. This is different from sin. Sin is a transgression of the law. There is a way God handles trespasses in Christ Jesus. He does not impute it unto you, He will not enter it to your account; rather it is accounted as already paid for by the sacrifice of Christ. This is what happens in Christ Jesus. So the first thing that happens to a man in Christ Jesus is the change in nature and imputation of righteousness. This happens instantly.

Now that you are in Christ, you are declared righteous because of what Jesus has done for you by his sacrifice on the cross and because of who you have become; the new creature born of the incorruptible word of God in the likeness of Christ after his image so stop those foolish efforts to establish your own righteousness.

'for being ignorant of the righteousness that God ascribes (which makes one acceptable to Him in word, thought and deed) and seeking to establish a righteousness (a means of salvation)of their own, they did not obey or submit themselves to God's righteousness' Rom. 10:3

This is what many believers who have been translated to the kingdom of Christ spend their life doing trying to establish their own righteousness based on rules and regulations. Personal efforts of such people have never and will never gain acceptability in God's sight. The problem is that they are ignorant of the righteousness God has ascribed to them when they believed. They want to labour to earn their own righteousness so they fast, they have a certain manner of speech, they have a certain dress style, and hairstyle etc. they become unsociable because they think these deeds make them acceptable to God. The only thing that makes them acceptable to God is the imputed righteousness by faith in Christ Jesus. It is the righteousness of grace by faith; you cannot earn it with your efforts. Righteous people live right but you cannot be a righteous person because you live right. So stop all those religiosity, all those self help and efforts that can never yield anything. Accept the righteousness of God that has been imputed to you, live in it, and manifest it to the world around you. Remember, it is a gift, you cannot earn a gift, and it is given by grace. You are not the righteous because of the things you do; you are the righteous because of who you are. Walk in this consciousness and cease all self help

CHAPTER 2

DO THE FIRST THING

''Like new born babies, you should crave (thirst for, earnestly desire) the pure (unadulterated) spiritual milk that by it, you may be nurtured and grow unto (completed) salvation'' I pet. 2:2

A certain time in my life, my family relocated from our home town to the city, it was my first time of being to the city, the vehicle that carried us was being directed by my dad who works in the city. When we got to the compound where our apartment was, the car stopped and we all got out, it was a three storey building and our flat was the third floor. It was my first time of being in an upstairs. So we followed the leading of my dad since he alone knew this place when we got to the apartment, we took so much time to explore it, entered the rooms, the bathroom, the toilets. We took a lot of time to walk in and out of the rooms, viewed the outside through the windows. Nobody concerned himself with the luggage that was still down; we just wanted to know the house and even much more, our way around the neighborhood.

When you are translated to this place called – in Christ Jesus- it is a different place from where you have been. It is a new kingdom where things are done differently from the way they are done in the kingdom of darkness where you have been. This is what qualifies you to be called a new born babe. You have absolutely no idea of what obtains in this kingdom at most; you will assume it is like where you are coming from. So you have the first important need of finding out what manner of place you have come, what kind of life is obtainable in this place, what privileges you have in this place, you should burn with an intense desire to know more about this realm called Christ Jesus that you have been translated to. This is the first thing you are expected to do.

Now in the kingdom of Christ, the only person that can give you the answer to any question you may have about the kingdom is the word of God – the bible. The reason why you should crave for the word of God is because it is the only way to know what has happened to you and the things God has prepared for you in Christ. It is the word that can tell you how you ought to live now in Christ, not just the observation of the people around you.

The people you see are at different stages and levels in their walk with God that is why you must not just look on them. It is the word that will teach you. You need to sincerely desire the enlightening word of God so that you can grow in knowledge and understanding of where you are. So when a man has come to Christ, the next thing he needs is the scriptures. The word of God is the blue print of the obtainable lifestyle of men in Christ Jesus. The scriptures not only tell us how to live but also teach us what privileges we have in Christ. The reason why many believers are still caged in the bondage of religion is because they never took time to search the scriptures after they believed to know what manner of place they have come and what is expected of them there. They just look around and try to copy the lifestyle of the people around them and imitate their behaviours. Such believers will always be carried to and fro by every wind of doctrine and the slights of men. They can never come to the place of conviction of anything. They are '' my pastor said – Christians'' they will always remain babes never attaining to the place of maturity in Christ. These are the worst kind of Christians because they are yet to start their journey in Christ. They retain their behaviour of old and have a copy of the new life.

Just like it is acceptable for every man to come into this world as a baby but never to remain like that after some years, it is also note worthy that you can come into the kingdom as a babe, having limited knowledge of what obtains and the affairs of the kingdom, but never to remain like that. It is the Father' desire to see you come to the place of fullness of statue and maturity in Christ where you are no longer a babe having limited knowledge of the Father's will and plans but have become his partner and co-laborer in his business, you cannot attain this by living – ''my pastor said kind of Christianity. You can only grow to fullness of stature by feeding; a baby doesn't need strong food to grow, all it requires is the mother's breast milk, however a stage comes when the mother's breast milk will not be enough for the baby's growth requirement, then grains start coming in to the baby's diet, eventually a stage will be reached where the baby requires enough energy to meet up with the many activity in the child and at this point, source of energy like carbohydrates becomes the baby's main food constituents. This also applies to a believer. As a babe, all you need to draw your daily nourishment is the sincere milk of the word of God. It has all you require for spiritual development at this stage, you don't need all those spiritual development at this stage, you don't need all those spiritual powers and miracles, it is kept at a later stage for you. Many of us have made such errors, you are just born again, and next you want to start working miracles, such can set the person up for destruction. Many people who ended up using magic in church also started that way. At the babe stage, you don't need power manifestation, the Holy Spirit in you will keep you and your Father will meet your need but you must feed on the word the only power manifestation you need is the deliverance from any sin or habit you had before you came to Christ. A stage comes after you have to feed and become established in knowledge about the kingdom and where you stand that you start to manifest the power of God. Your walk in Christ is in stages but when people don't want to do what their stage requires but are looking at another person who is at another stage, you begin to leapfrog and that is not allowed. Live your life in Christ each stage at a time, don't desire to jump because there are vital work to be done at each stage and an important lesson to learn which you will need at the stages ahead. If you neglect a stage for another, you set yourself up for a big trouble when the challenges come.

Dr. Tunde Bakare always says *''A new level brings a new devil, that there is a devil at every level you must conquer.* So if you jumped a level, it means in addition to the devil in that new level, the devil you have not defeated in the level you jumped will be added to it. It is a stepwise walk.

After I came to Christ many years ago, the first intense desire I always had was the desire to manifest the power in the Name of Jesus. This was after seeing great men of God who are in a stage far ahead of where I was. Yet, that became an intense desire in me for many years. I tried but it will not always work as I wanted till God one day brought me to the understanding that ''How do you expect to control that which is the Father's when you have not grown up to be like the Father/there are a lot of character defects and instability yet you want the Father's all??

''Now I say that the heir, as long as he is a child differenth nothing from a servant, though he be lord of all. But is under tutors and governors until time appointed by the Father, even so we, when we were children, were in bondage under the elements of the world '' Gal. 4:1-3

An heir is someone that is entitled to a possession he/she does not need to work to get, but his/her entitlement is as a result of who he/she is. No matter how great an inheritance reserved for a heir could be, no matter how intense the desire he/she may have to take over the Father's business, if he is not mature, he cannot have it. In the legal world, a boy that is below 18years will still be called a minor and at such age is not expected to make any decision legally when not guided by the parents or mentor. In the realm of the spirit, maturity is not a question of the number of years one has been born again, it is not a question of how many activities in the church one attains or how you have followed faithfully your church doctrine, maturity rather is a question of how much of you is yielded to the will of God. How much of the Father you have become. In the world the more you are able to make a decision and stand the consequences of your decision the more mature you are becoming, but in Christ Jesus, the more you can leave your own decisions and look on the Father depending on Him for everything you do, the more mature you have become. The more you learn to please God more than yourself, the more mature you have become. The key to walking in all the Father has for you on earth is hidden in the word of God that is why it must be your greatest companion. In Christ, you are not entitled to anything you have not discovered. It is what you can see that you can possess so when you see through the word of God, all God has prepared for you, you receive the capacity to walk in these things also, but if you are looking around at what people around you are doing, you will find yourself struggling in your walk with God.

After I received Christ as my Lord and Saviour, I was translated to become a new creature according to what the bible said. I expected some things I struggled with before to leave me, but they didn't, I was a very shy person, I couldn't stand a crowd, I had a strong stage fright that followed me to Christ for about 2 years I came to Christ, I couldn't witness to anybody because of that, even though I had a strong burden in my heart and I continued to pray about it every day I even fasted and asked God to help me and grant me boldness just like the apostles did when they were threatened with fear by the Pharisees, but I did not receive the boldness I desired, it was until God showed me a scripture in 2 Tim. 1:7 that He has not given me the spirit of fear, but of love, power and of a sound mind. I began to say that and pray with it and I tell you when fear left me, I could not even notice. I just discovered I can stand and preach even in a bus or church or street. This is because what you have not discovered, you cannot experience. Rev. David Ogbueli once said that the limitation of the church is not the limitation of prayer but the limitation of revelation. This is because we no longer desire the sincere milk of the word of God, we prefer the word of men which cannot give us the foundation of faith we need. The men that have championed the revivals that have hit the church in the generations past are people who had that foundation of faith on the word of God, not on the word of preachers.
After the conversion of Paul, He did not immediately run to Jerusalem which was the headquarter of the church then where Apostles Peter, James, John etc were, he went to Arabia where he spent three years learning of God according to the scriptures, it was a time to know what God has said concerning him, it was a time to be taught by God. Paul at this time desired the sincere milk of the word to know the mind of the Father for him Gal. 1:16-18

This is the pattern according to the scriptures when you come to Christ, the first thing you need is the word not what men think or understand you need to desire the sincere word, the scriptures the little way you can understand it. You need a lot of personal study of the word not your group bible study. When I came to Christ, I couldn't even recite John 3:16, I could not as much as say anything in the scriptures meanwhile, I had been going to church all the while. I discovered a new desire to put the scriptures in my heart. I always read my bible before I study my books in school, pick verses and try to put them in memory, I discovered a lot of things within this period that got me praying for myself, some habits I enjoyed and found contrary to the God's will for my life, which I didn't need anybody to preach to me to stop. This is the first thing, this is what God expects of you even after you attend church or fellowship, take the things the pastor has said and study it again, reading all the scriptures he quoted to understand. Many people will take as scripture out of context to make a point but if you do not inspect such message, you will end up in error. It is not bad to check even Paul after preaching, the people went back to check whether the things he said were so, it is not doubt, it is just being sure before you let things into your spirit.

CHAPTER 3

UNDERSTAND YOUR CALLING

''...But a He which has called you is holy, so be ye holy in all manner of conversation, because it is written, be ye Holy, for I Am Holy'' I Pet. 1: 15-16

In Christ, you have been called into holiness; you have been called to live a holy life. It is not a suggestion, it is a lifestyle, and you are required to live in word and deed in holiness. The ground upon which God makes this request of a holy living on his people is because He is holy. Our God is the most Holy God, and if we will walk with him, we must be holy also, it is also important to know that in Christ Jesus, you have been recreated in the image and likeness of the son of God; hence you have all it takes to fulfill this demand of God over your life. When we were dead and buried in sin, God never raised a demand to live holy because the equipment was not given, but in Christ Jesus the nature of sin has been taken away and replaced with the nature of righteousness hence you can now live a holy life, just as the one who has called you is a holy God. But then what really does it mean to live a holy life? What is holiness? Is it a way of speech or a manner of dressing, it is an appearance or an attitude; it is all about dos and don'ts, is holiness the same thing as self denial or self abasement? Is it a physical exercise or a spiritual virtue? Is holiness an attitude I should exhibit only when I come to the presence of God or in the midst of God's people? What does God mean when He called us to holiness? Is it a calling to a pattern of dressing or avoiding certain pleasures? Is it just not wearing earrings? Is holiness dressing unattractive as old fashion? Is it living a life of legalism without power? Is holiness all about abstinence from things to gain heaven's acceptance? At different points in the life of the church, men have misunderstood this calling to be merely just an activity or an appearance, but it is much more than that. Remember that our calling to holiness is because God Himself is holy, so we are learning holiness from the Father. When God said '' I Am Holy'', Does it mean He has a particular dress code, or activity He engages Himself in? Is He saying He is abstaining from the works of His hands? Does it mean he stays away from the beauty that His own hands made? For a long time, I struggled with the teaching of holiness that discourages people taking care of themselves and looking good for God. I believed our God is glorious and the splendor of His glory is much more than one can imagine, yet He is a Holy God. Holiness is not just an appearance or a mere activity or pattern of behavior, holiness is God's way of life, it is what has made God to remain who He is after generations unending. Holiness is God's fragrance.

WHAT THEN IS HOLINESS?

For us to understand holiness, we must never take it away from God. It is from God we can see what holiness really is and then apply it to our own context. This is because holiness did not originate from man, neither is it man's idea, it is God's way of life, His fragrance, and we are only called to walk in this path with Him.

Now holiness is God's way of life, of having the power to do all things – both Good and bad, yet choosing to do only the right things. Holiness is God's check on His power, He can do anything, anytime, anyhow but He chooses to follow the laws He has set to govern the universe.

Holiness is what God uses to balance His unlimited power if I can put it that way. Now I have not been in the place of absolute power before but I have had authority given me to exercise over others and I have come to understand that power intoxicates, absolute power intoxicates absolutely. The reason why

God is still in control and not overwhelmed by the absolute power He has is because He is holy. He made a choice to use it for the benefit of creation. It was Job who spoke that God has the power to kill and make alive, yet some religious folks will say God does not kill; but my question to such people is – who killed the first born of the Egyptians? God's power is absolute, yet He chooses to use it for the benefit of creation, this is holiness.

Now for all who has been born again who has been translated in Christ, we have been brought into the place of liberty of the sons of God in Christ Jesus; It is a place where Paul declared that all things are lawful for me but not all things are beneficial, a place where your sins have been forgiven you by the sacrifice of Jesus and the Lord does not impute trespasses on His people because of the sacrifice of Jesus. This is a place of liberty indeed and this is why God called us to holiness. Holiness now becomes our check on our liberty in Christ

Now that we have the knowledge of good and evil, holiness is a call for us to always choose to do the right thing with our liberty in Christ Jesus. Holiness is not just being so conscious of sin that you begin to live a legalistic life, rather it is being very conscious of righteousness that you begin to live a life of the spirit. For us, holiness is a lifestyle not a dressing or appearance or attitude. It is a taking away of your appetite for sin and all its offers to righteousness and godliness. What holiness will do in the life of a believer is that it will make you turn away from sin not because of yourself or what people will say, but because we have an appetite for righteousness so we go for it.

If I know that when I enter a mud and play in it so that I become as dirty as a pig, that if I enter the shower and bath, I will be clean again, it is possible for me to make the mud my playing ground, after which I can always have a bath. However, a higher level of maturity is when I know that the mud will get me dirty and I avoid it because I don't want to dirty, so I don't play in it, even though the shower can always wash me clean again. This second opinion is the real implication of holiness; this is a little illustration of holiness. Many of us having understood that God has promised forgiveness of sin in Christ Jesus, could just choose to live anyhow after all I can always ask for forgiveness and I will get it. However holiness will teach you to avoid doing those things that will get your garment stained even though the blood of Jesus can blot out any stain, because you know the Father wants you to be pure for Him.

So holiness is having the ability to do evil yet by choice setting your capacity only on doing good no matter what.

It is not just turning from sin because of your personality or what people will say if you get caught in your sin, it is turning from sin because of God, because it won't please God whom your whole desire is just to please. It is not something that just happens; it is something you determine to do because of your love for the Lord, because you have realized that it is not about yourself but about the Father. This is because you have understood that your liberty is not just given you to do as you please, but to help you please the Father always, in Gen. 39:7-9 (GNB)

Joseph was well built and good looking, and after a while his master's wife began to desire him and ask him to go to bed with her. He refused and said to her ''look, my master does not have to concern himself with anything in the house, because I am here. He has put me in charge of everything he has. I have as much authority in this house as he has and he has not kept back anything from me exc4ept you. How could I do such an immoral thing and sin against God''

What Potiphar's wife demanded of Joseph was not beyond the reach of Joseph, he could as well use the liberty the master has given him to sleep with the master's wife but he had understanding that the liberty was not given him to misbehave but for service, for effective service, secondly, he was not even concerned with what the master will do if he found out, he did such a thing because this will be the first concern of most of us, he was concerned about how he would displease God if he accepted the offer. Joseph had the ability to attain to his master's wife evil intentions, but he chose not to because it won't please God, this is holiness. It is choosing to be on the Lord's side with your liberty of choice at all times no matter the options. You cannot operate in this dimension of holiness except you come to the following–

1. You have come to love the Father because of the great love He has showered on us, that you have set your heart at all times to please Him. Your desire to express your love to God is one thing that will help you walk in holiness not just church doctrine or what people could say if you do otherwise.

2. That the liberty of the sons of God is given them for effective service in the Father's kingdom, not for them to live carelessly. You must understand that grace is not a license to live as you like rather it is an empowerment to live as you should.

When these two understandings become fully established in our hearts, then it becomes very easy to walk in this dimension of holiness.

Secondly, holiness is a pursuit of righteousness not just a fleeing from sin. It is not just an abstinence from sin but much more the clinging to righteousness.

Many times, our teachings on holiness have always focused on abstinence from sin, from things that defiles us. This has put people in more danger of temptation of that which they are running away from. People that ran away from sin always had sin overpower them in their weakest moments that most of them never recovered from the fall. Holiness is our only way to have victory over sin. It is the pursuit of righteousness that is by faith in the sacrifice of Jesus Christ thereby putting us in the opposite direction to sin. No man in the pursuit of righteousness have time to mingle with sin rather the pursuit of righteousness will clear from our minds any room for sin and deliver us from false holiness and make us sons of the kingdom living a holy life like our Father. Holiness focuses on what to cling to not just on what to abstain from. Except your walk of holiness produces righteousness, it is not holiness; it could have been a practice of doctrine. Most people have been satisfied just abstaining from things they were pointed to and told to be sin, without making any effort to cling to righteousness, such people have not really understood holiness.

Flee the evil desires of youth and pursue righteousness, faith, love and peace, along with those who call on the Lord out of a pure heart. 2Tim 2:22 NIV

Holiness is not just abstaining from sexual immoralities or alcohol, it is about clinging to the doctrine of Christ. It is the pursuit after righteousness that takes us far away from sin and all its desires. It is the desire to please God (by living right and doing what is expected of us by God) that destroys every desire to please self and flesh in us. Holiness is the life pattern of God's people here on earth. It is not just about abstaining from the works of the flesh, lying, fornication, adultery, lust, envy, hatred, strife etc. rather it is manifesting the life of the spirit which is love, joy, peace, longsuffering, gentleness, goodness, faith meekness, temperance. It is not just an abstinence from sin, rather a pursuit of righteousness. God is Spirit and his life style is holiness. If we live by the spirit, we manifest the life patterns of God. When we manifest the fruits of the spirit; this is holiness. This is our calling in Christ Jesus, Holiness is not a way of speech, rather its God's way of thinking, Holiness is not a form of appearance, it is God's pattern of life. Holiness is not an activity but God's lifestyle. Holiness does not make us unattractive and old fashioned, it makes us the centre of attraction of all men, Holiness is not a man's idea, and it is Gods purpose for His children. Holiness is not a choice; Holiness is Heaven's expectation on the saints. It is our calling in Christ Jesus. BE YE HOLY FOR I AM HOLY.

THE MAIN FOCUS OF HOLINESS

The real focus of holiness is not just to change the physical outlook of God's people from the world, but to transform our minds. The starting point of Holiness is our minds, our labour to control the evil thoughts that run through the heart of man. This is the first labour of Holiness. After the fall of man in the garden, God testified that every thought that went on in the heart of man was evil continuously. Holiness is a way of changing our thoughts from the fallen man to the recreated man in Christ Jesus. All our labour to change our physical looks without changing our inside will only end up setting us up for a greater trouble. If you keep on laboring to detest the attire and certain dress code in the world without first laboring to change your mind, putting righteousness at the mother board of your heart, you will struggle to experience the liberty of holiness and end up enslaving yourself to men. You will see yourself come to the place where you need people to be around for you to behave and this is nothing different from the way of life of the Pharisees. The right order is for us to first establish our minds in righteousness which the ripple effect will manifest in our appearance, attitude and behavior without struggle. The key to living a holy life is thinking like God thinks.

''Let the wicked forsake his ways and the unrighteous man his thoughts and let him return unto the Lord and he will have mercy upon him and on our God for He will abundantly pardon'' Isa. 55:7

God speaking through the prophets in this scripture was laying a foundation and pattern to follow in or walk of holiness. The scriptures boldly declare that the wicked should turn from his ways, not the acts of his wickedness. The ways of the wicked is that evil seed in him that make him devise wicked devices to carry out his wicked acts. It is like an evil script written in the heart of the wicked man; these acts are just his wicked actions that he exhibits towards others, so the labour of holiness is for us to change that evil script writer, that evil seed inventing evil devices in men. This can only happen when we begin to meditate on God's word and change our thought factory with God's word.

The scripture also said the unrighteous man should forsake his thoughts. This is because the real thing that makes us righteous before God is our thought not our appearance just as what makes people unrighteous is their thoughts. This is why all these efforts people put in to change their appearance, if they put in same effort to changing their thought life, it will yield far much fruit of holiness than the legalism of hypocrisy all around. We like to emphasize greatly the need for people to dress properly but we emphasize very little or even not at all on the need to be transformed in our thoughts. We are more conscious of taking charge of the world around us than confronting the world within us; but except we are able to take charge of the world within, we cannot be relevant in the world around us.

WHAT THEN ARE THOUGHTS

Thoughts are motivators for action. They are the things that lead one to do the things he/she does. Thoughts are not seen, but every action a man takes has its origin from thoughts. So for every action there is a motivator, if we fight the actions, without taking care of the motivation, it will be a useless fight.

Now before any man take a conscious peep into the breast of a woman, in his mind there is a motivator painting a picture of what he could see and encouraging him to just take that one look; then he peeps. If all we do is to fight the act and not the motivator, it is like cutting the stem of a tree without stumping it, it's only a matter of time the tree will come back to life.

When man fell, God testified that the motivator of man's actions continually was evil and after you come to Christ, the mind, the motivator of your actions must be reset to righteousness and that is the work of holiness. All this energy put to changing appearance should rather be channeled to changing the motivator of your actions now you are in Christ. This is not automatic, this is a conscious effort and you must choose to think the way God thinks to walk the way He does.

Finally, brethren, whatsoever things are true, whatsoever things are honest, whatsoever things are just, whatsoever things are pure, whatsoever things are lovely, whatsoever things are of good report, if there be any virtue and if there be any praise. Think on these Phil 4:6

As a child of God called to be holy by the will of the Father, we must change our motivation of action to those things Paul highlighted in this scripture. We must replace our motivator of action from evil to be truth, honesty, purity, love, good report, virtue and praise. These things should rule our thoughts if we want to operate in God's kind of holiness that brings liberty. It means that when thoughts begin to rise within you and you weigh it on the scale of the scriptures and it falls short, terminate such thought and deny it ability to express itself in action. It will take a while but before you know it becomes a way of life for you. When you change your thought pattern to be in line with the scriptures, it will influence your speech life and actions too and you will operate in the nature of God whether people are around or not. You will find out that just the same way it is easy to live in sin and wickedness when we were in the world, it is also easy to live holy and righteous before God in Christ Jesus.

Holiness begins from the mind not just from your appearance. What you wear or don't wear does not approve you before God, it is how much of Him you have become in thought and in walk, that makes you holy. Holiness is God's calling, His lifestyle and no man can know holiness more than God. Let the wicked man forsake his ways and the unrighteous man his thoughts and let them come to the Lord. You cannot come to God and pursue righteousness and not forsake the way of sin. The best way to be far from sin is by pursuing after righteousness, not just by running away from sin. The only way to change your thought is by recreating it in line with the word of God. This is why the scripture teaches us to be transformed by renewing our minds with God's word, because the more you behold God in His word; the more you are transformed to be like God

Let not your life of holiness be a futile struggle with the change of appearance and speech, let it be the recreation of the man within, the changing of appetite from sin to righteousness , let it be a decision to do the right thing in the sight of God no matter the choices and challenges it may bring . Let your holiness be greater than that of the Pharisees else it is a labour in vain

For I say unto you that except your righteousness exceeds the righteousness of the Scribes and Pharisees, you shall in no case enter into the kingdom of heaven (Matt. 5:20)

CHAPTER 4

UNDERSTANDING GRACE

"*For the Grace of God that brings salvation has appeared to all men, training us to renounce ungodliness and worldly passions and to live self – controlled, upright and godly lives in this present age:* Titus 2: 11 - 12 (KJV)

Grace has been one of the subjects in the Christian faith that has been wildly misunderstood. A lot of people have taught on this subject as a way to explain what it really means and why a believer needs a close walk with Grace, but end up confusing the people and getting them yield to the fleshy lust within our flesh. A lot of people have tried to give a definition to grace to help the believer understand it a little more. Over the years we have had definition like Grace meaning God in your race. Some said it means unmerited favour. All these are idea of Grace that scratch the barrel but not really going on the full understanding of it. One thing you have to understand is that Grace came from the Lord Jesus Himself. You cannot take Grace away from God, Grace only exist when looking at God's relationship with man. Between men there is no such thing as grace. Grace is of God. It is an act of God that makes God condescend to still relate to man; but much more bring man up to where He is.

GRACE IS NOT LAW

For the law was given through Moses, grace and truth came through Jesus Christ. John 1:17

Grace and law are not the same neither do they look alike. They do not achieve the same purpose nor were they intended to. Some people see Grace and law as two roads that lead to the same place, but the truth is that they are not. Grace and law are like water and oil, no matter what you can do, you cannot get a homogenous solution of the two. They are immiscible; they cannot blend with one another.

From the introduction of the Law through Moses as the scripture has said, the law was given as a school master. It's assignment was to show man what he really is without God, to prove to the most righteous man that without God he is helpless. The law was given to man to show man how far he has fallen since after the fall of man, to reveal how evil every intention of man's heart has become. To show man that he has evil tendencies which he may not believe. The law was given to show man that he is a natural sinner without God. The limitation of the law was that it revealed the state of man and the wickedness in the heart of man but it offers no solution. The law is like a therapy given to one who was informed of having terminal disease, the intention is never to cure but to manage the sickness, to help prolong the life of the person. The law was never going to save man from his fallen state of sin but was just to help him manage the problem of sin till salvation comes.

LAW EXPIRED WHEN GRACE WAS REVEALED

The law was never given for us to keep it; even God knew man could not keep it. In fact, the scripture said it was impossible for any man to please God just by keeping the law. God does not like the law in the first place because it reminds Him of man's fall. So how can I please God by doing the things He hates so well? The law was given for us to see how difficult it is to fulfill God's demand. The law was introduced for me to see my sins and to see how much I need God in my life.

''why then was the law given? It was given alongside the promise to show people their sins. But the law was designed to last only until the coming of the child who was the mediator between God and the people'' Gal. 3:19 (NLT)

The law was not given as a remedy to sin, but as a school master, to guide man, to keep man in check in his fallen state till the promise of deliverance from sin was fulfilled. It is like a drug given to an AIDS patient to still keep him alive till the promise cure or healing he/she is anticipating arrives. The law could not save even a man that keeps it 100% even though none was ever accounted to have done so. But if it were that men could keep the law a 100%, they will yet not be saved from the wrath of God, neither will they be reconciled to God. God gave us the law to show us how much we have fallen and how much of Him we really need. But in the agenda of God, the law ended with the fulfillment of the promise of a messiah fulfilled.

''Do not think that I have come to abolish the law or the prophets; I have not come to abolish them but to fulfill them'' Matt. 5:12 ESV

"To fulfill," mean to achieve the thing you hoped for or wished, it also means to provide what is necessary or needed, it also means to conclude or bring something to an end. Jesus came that the Father may achieve what He planned from the foundation of the world, the salvation of mankind not by law. He came to provide that which the law was lacking regarding the saving of souls from sin. Jesus in order to provide what we needed to connect man back to the Father brought Grace. Jesus came to conclude the dispensation of law and start a new and better way back to the Father. Grace is not another law but it is a better covenant. It is not a license to sin as many who misunderstood it have taught rather it is a deliverance from sin and sinful nature. Grace does not tell you ''do not do this!'' it rather teaches you the things you should do. Grace is of our Lord Jesus Christ. Grace is from God.

WHAT THEN IS GRACE?

Grace can be said to be God's all at Christ expenses. It is an expression of Gods kindness and favour under the new covenant with Jesus Christ as the mediator. Grace is a divine exchange where Jesus took from us everything that we have ever done wrong in exchange for all he has done well and ask the Father to put on us every benefit that belongs to him. It is Jesus taking our place and giving us his place of favour and love with the Father. Grace is God reconciling man to Himself, blotting away every offense and gilt record against him and giving him a fresh chance to walk with Him. It is God reaching out to man and giving him an opportunity to walk with Him again. From the fall of man, man became an enemy of God, but when grace was revealed, God broke the wall of enemy in search of man not to condemn him again because he was already condemned, but to deliver him from sin and reconcile him back to Himself. Grace comes through Jesus Christ; it is God qualifying you not because of your qualification but because of your faith in the sacrifice of Jesus on the cross. Grace is God's solution to man's problem. It is the solution to the sinful nature of man which the law revealed. Grace brought solution to man's struggle with sin by changing the nature of sin in man. It offers you an opportunity to start afresh. Grace formats the heart of man; removing everything that sin has deposited there and gives you an opportunity for a fresh start. This is one wonderful thing about grace, it does not just reveal your state of heart, but it changes your pattern of life and thought

''if any man be in Christ, He is a new creature, old things are passed away, behold all things are become new'' 2Cor. 5:17

Grace gives a fresh start to everyman, where you do not have to blame Adam for his disobedience any more. It offers a fresh walk with God with all events of the past blotted away by the blood of Jesus and forgotten. For you to have a fruitful walk of grace, you must know that yesterday is past and gone. You must first get the revelation of the new creature.

THE REVELATION OF THE NEW CREATURE

Whenever the word ''new'' is mentioned it's because there was before then something that existed called ''old'' when we come into the covenant of grace which Jesus is the mediator, the first revelation we must understand is that you have become a new creature. It is not that you will become a new creature when the work of grace is done! No! You from the moment you acknowledge the Lordship of Jesus and submit your life to his sacrifice for sin on the cross, you obtain the status of the new creature. It means a new you have just been born, with new desires, new abilities and capabilities. It means your spirit man has been recreated in Christ Jesus; that nature of sin; that evil magnet that always draws a sinner to sin is no longer found in this you that has been born. You received the capacity to say no to sin and yes to righteousness. It means in the sight of God, He sees a brand new you as new as it has never been before. This is the reality of what happens at salvation when we get born again.

The second event that we must understand in the revelation of the new creature is "... Old things are passed away'' this means that the error of the past is gone away from you. The sins of the past have been forgiven and taken away from you. It means you have been acquitted of any wrong of your past. Satan has no right to torment you with events from the past anymore. In the human court of law, when a man is acquitted of any crimes, you cannot hold that crime against him anymore even if he is guilty as charged or you find fresh evidence to prove his guilt. Here old things refer to the events of your past, the mistakes of your pasts. They are erased away. They are no longer valid evidence against you in God's court of justice.

Old things are passed away also means that the old ways of doing things, your old way of life and living has become obsolete. It means you should not return to your old pattern of life. You should not go back to have fellowship with the unfruitful works of darkness. It means you have just been reprogrammed and now runs on a different operating system.

However, many people go back to locate those old patterns of life and begin to live them again. You are living an obsolete life, it is like eating an expired food, no matter how sweet it was before going stale/bad, you can never enjoy it anymore instead it causes sickness and disease to your body. Old things are passed away, so you leave the old in the past. You seek to know the new pattern of life to follow.

Thirdly, you need to realize the most interesting work of grace which is the making of all things new. You cannot get to that place where all things have become new if you don't understand the revelation of the new creature and that old things have passed away, when the old have passed away, you should not hold it in high regards again or allow it interfere with the present. You just leave it in the past and walk in your present.

GRACE, YOUR NEW TEACHER

''for the grace of God that bringeth salvation hath appeared to all men, teaching us that denying ungodliness and worldly lust, we should live soberly, righteously and godly in this present world; looking for that blessed hope and the glorious appearing of the great God and our savior Jesus Christ''. Titus 2:11-13

I have heard a lot of people talk about grace and they say it is all about what Jesus did and nothing you can do. That at best is a half truth. Grace is of the Lord Jesus, but when grace comes it teaches. The initiation of grace, the returning home of the prodigal son and the Father's acceptance is the beginning of grace, but his conduct afterwards will be from the experience he has gotten. Grace is what brought us back to God when Jesus paid the price for our sins, but when grace of God was revealed, it did not reconcile man back to God so that man will return to do those things God hates just after the reconciliation. Grace abounded much more to teach God's people how to live now having been reconciled to God. Grace is not a license for sin or lawlessness, though there is no law in grace but we are guided by the law of the spirit of life in Christ Jesus. It is not the law of sin and death. The work of grace is to teach us how to take on a God-filled, God honouring life. If you have found the grace of our Lord Jesus Christ, not as though you found it, but grace found you, then it will teach you how to live to please God. When you were in the world, you lived to please the flesh and its desires but now grace teaches us how to live to please the Father to whom we have been reconciled. If the grace you know is just a liberty to do anything you like after all Christ paid in full, you have lost it. You are at best walking in self delusion and self deceit.

Grace is not law, but the deliverance from sin and its nature

Grace will teach you to deny ungodliness and worldly lust. Ungodliness is the act of walking contrary to the known way of God. Not living like God, or following His ways and pattern of doing things. **If you know what God requires of you but you do your own thing instead, that is ungodliness.** Worldly lust is an intense desire to please the flesh which dominates the life of people in the world. It has its root in selfishness. In the world people live as they like and do what they please, not minding what God says about it. Everyone is in a race to satisfy their flesh but in Christ it is not so.. This is what grace teaches us. It teaches us how to follow God fully by following His known will for our life and helps us overcome that intense desire to satisfy the flesh and its desires rather than to satisfy God; so that all you want to do is to please God with your life. If you must be fruitful in your walk of grace, you must learn how to deny ungodliness and worldliness and worldly lust. Grace alone can teach you how.

HOW GRACE TEACHES

''For it is God which worketh in you both to will and to do of His good pleasure'' Phil 2:13

One outstanding difference between law and grace is that the law shows you what not to do, but cannot teach you how not to do that, but grace tells you what to do and teaches or empowers you to go ahead and do that. Grace teaches us the things that the Father requires of us as his reconciled children and enables us by the power of the Holy Ghost to do these things. The power of the Holy Spirit is the only enablement that a believer has to please God. Anyone who wants to please the Father without the presence and person of the Holy Spirit will not succeed because no man can please God. God has to please Himself in us through the Holy Spirit. The scripture we read above said it is God that works in us to will i.e. God tells us what he requires from us through His word written in the bible or proceeding word and he also gives us the ability to do what he has shown us to be his requirement through the Holy Spirit. This is how grace teaches. It shows us what the will of God is and gives us the enablement by the Holy Spirit to do it. It is an empowerment to do the will of God that we have known. In the law it is not like that. So grace is not a ticket to live as we want, but an encouragement to live as we should. Let us try to understand this from one of the parables of our Lord Jesus Christ.

The kingdom of heaven is like unto a certain king, who made a marriage for his son and sent forth his servant to call them that were bidden to the wedding and they would not come. Again, he sent forth other servants, saying tell them which are bidden, behold I have prepared my dinner. My oxen and my fatlings are killed and all things are ready, come unto the marriage but they made light of it, and went their ways, one to his farm, another to his merchandise; and the remnant took his servants and entreated them spitefully and slew them. But when the king heard thereof, he was wroth and he sent forth his armies and destroyed those murderers and burned up their city then said he to his servant; the wedding is ready, but they which were bidden were not worthy, go ye therefore into the highways, and as many as you shall find , bid to the marriage.

So those servants went out into the high ways and gathered together on many and they found, both bad and good and the wedding was furnished with guests and when the king came in to see the guests, he saw a man which had no wedding garment: and he said unto him ,friend, how comest thou in hither not having a wedding garment? And he was speechless. Then said the king to the servants, bind him hand and foot and take away and cast him unto outer darkness, there shall be weeping and gnashing of teeth. For many are called but few are chosen". Matthew 22:2-14.

The first time I read this parable, I was totally confused at the action of the king. He sent his servants to the high way to bid anyone they see to come to the wedding, for all things are now ready, yet the king came in and seeing a man not dressed for the party, he cast him into outer darkness where there will be weeping and gnashing of teeth.

When I had not understood the work of grace, I found this action of this King in the parable wrong because the man was not pre- informed of any party before leaving his home, so why should he be thus judged?

This parable tells us the work of grace; God called Abraham and made a covenant with him and his children forever. By this covenant, Israel became a special people on earth but like the people invited for the feast, they had excuses to give to God why they are not ready for him. Jesus came but they rejected him as they rejected the servants sent to tell them about the banquet. God now reached out to the entire world, calling anybody anywhere. This is grace. People who afore time where not accepted to God are not called into his banquet. But the reality is that this parable is an illustration of our redemption in Christ and how we were grafted in to God's plan with no pre information. Grace was on the streets calling out to all men to come for God is no longer angry with us and He has broken the wall of separation that our sins had raised. This indeed is true but when you answer the invitation of grace, you must allow grace teach you how you must live now that you have been reconciled to God. Grace does not deny preparation it only guarantees invitation when you were not qualified and having been invited, it is necessary you prepare to answer the call. I believe the people were told where the banquet was going to hold of which the man knew he cannot appear before the king with filthy rags. This is a dimension of grace people talk less of- the teaching dimension of grace. Grace gives the invitation and teaches us what to do to answer the call. Grace teaches us that denying ungodliness and worldliness, we should live soberly, righteously and godly in this present world.

If the grace you have found always tells you to come as you are but does not also teach you about denials and the things to cling to, then it is not a full package of Grace. The same way the people were invited to the king's bouquet that is how you and I are called into the place of the beloved.

However, if you will not be a cast away, you must allow grace to teach you how to dress, how to behave and what to cling unto in this calling of grace. Grace is not liberty to sin, but a choice to live righteously before God. This parable will be fulfilled at the appearing of Christ, when many people born again by altar call will appear before the throne, but did not allow grace to have his perfect work in their life, they thought grace is a license to sin at Christ's expense; they will receive the same judgment given to that servant. For many are called by Grace, but just few allow grace to teach them the way of the kingdom, only those are chosen for the Father's bouquet.

CHAPTER 5

THE POWER OF PRAYER

"The earnest (heart felt, continued) prayer of a righteous man makes tremendous power available (dynamic in its working)" James 5:16 (Amp)

Prayer is one of the most engaged activities in the 21st century church. Some people even believe it is the answer to every problem. It is also called the master key of life though it is not, most of the gatherings in the church today are prayer meeting and prayer ministries are springing up everywhere. Yet in the midst of all these, a lot of people are gradually losing faith in prayer.

A lot of people who pray do not believe the prayer will be answered and many more people are gradually losing faith in the power and potency of prayer. We see a lot of people using charm in the church today to perform miracles because they do not know how to harness the power of God through prayer. The more we are praying, the more people are losing faith in prayer. Now does it mean God no longer answers prayer? Or the power of prayer had finally been depleted? For us to answer this question, we need to understand the meaning of prayer.

Prayer is a communion with God through the Holy Spirit. It is a communication with God in which the people of God express their heart to the Father in words, emotions and or songs. It is not only the words you speak after you say "in Jesus name". Prayer is every communication that proceeds out of your heart.

As a child of God filled with the Holy Spirit, you are always connected to the Father so also he to you hence there is always communication. Prayer is all about the earth reaching to heaven and the heaven responding to the earth just like the dream Jacob had where a ladder went up from the earth to the heaven and he saw Angels ascending and descending on it. Prayer is such a relationship, the ladder we have is the Holy Spirit, He connect us to the Father directly so that there is always activities ascending and descending.

A lot of people think prayer is just when you kneel down and close your eyes and put your hands together, and begin to speak, prayer is much more than that. It is a transmission of information from earth to heaven and heaven to the earth. The most important components of prayer is the Holy Spirit. It is not the loudness of our prayer that makes the Father hear it even the best speakers on earth cannot transmit up to 30km into the atmosphere. It is not about shouting your prayer point but the Holy Spirit. The Holy Spirit searches our heart; He transmits the things we pray for to the Father. The Holy Spirit in you is like the handset you carry about. If you have one, you can communicate with someone over 100km away from you with a cool tone or voice. You do not need to shout or raise your voice. So the Holy Spirit in us helps us to pray to the Father. He transmits our prayer to the Father's ear, not the loudness of our voice.

"And in the same way, by our faith, the Holy Spirit helps us with our daily problems and in our praying. For we don't even know what we should pray for nor how to pray as we should, but the Holy Spirit prays for us with such feeling that it cannot be expressed in words. And the Father who knows all hearts knows, of course, what the spirit is saying as he pleads for us in hamming with God's own will." (Rom 8:26-27 TLB)

It is the Holy Spirit that transmits our prayers to the Father, hence any man who has not the Spirit of God in him cannot pray. At best you speak word, but no one to bring your words to the Father's ear. The scripture says we do not even know how to pray, the right emotional expressions and the right words to say if we were to speak for ourselves before the Father, but the Holy Spirit intercedes i.e. he take that which we have asked of God and properly presents it to God on our behalf. He even expresses the feeling of our infirmity to God and God who knows what the spirit is saying will respond to our prayer. So you can agree with me that the Holy Spirit is very important in prayer; in fact the most important component of prayer that produces result.

Another important component of prayer is what we say and do in prayer. This involves the words we speak in the place of prayer, the emotions we express, our sighs, groans. Prayer does not only involve words, also what we say by your action, by body language, emotions and states of heart as we commune with God. This speaking aspect is also a reason why people do not get result out of their prayer. When your word of prayer is contrary to what you are speaking by your other forms of speaking, you cannot have what you have prayed for. In fact you will have what you say by your other forms of speaking than just what you utter by words to God. This is because what your action says means more to God than your word is saying.

"For verily I say unto you, that whosoever shall say unto this mountain be than removed and be than cast into the sea, and shall not doubt in his heart. But shall believe that those things which he saith shall come to pass, He shall have whatsoever he saith" Mark 11:23-24.

Many times we say a word of prayer and afterwards speak a different thing by our actions and because our actions always speak louder, that which we have said in prayer becomes defeated. Prayer must be a unity of words and action. You must say the same thing. Remember prayer is more than just kneeling down and folding your hands, the Holy Spirit keeps the lines open all the time so everything you say, every sigh you make, every groan is a prayer because it is communicated by the Spirit to the Father. That is why we should speak the right words all the time; our actions must say the right things that our word of prayer is saying for us to have the answer we desire.

For instance, a woman who wants to get pregnant to have a child but every one week to the end of her menstrual cycle she buys a pad, she will have what she says. The action says she is expecting her menstruation rather than pregnancy and because the expectation of the righteous shall not be cut short, God will give her what she says. This disagreement between our words of prayer and what our action says is one of the things that is robbing people of the power of prayer

HOW CAN I BE EFFECTIVE IN PRAYER

The heartfelt continued prayer of a righteous man makes tremendous power available (dynamic in action).

This statement was extracted from James 5:16(Amp). The ingredients of an effective prayer can be gotten from this verse of scripture. First of all, an effective prayer is one that makes tremendous power available and brings result at the end of the day. The bible is filled with stories of people who prayed effective prayer and obtained undeniable results in their time. When we look back to the Old Testament up till the time of the apostles even in this generation we still have people who prayed effective prayers and obtained result. For example Peter and John at the beautiful gate prayed for a man who was cripple and he immediately rose up and walked into the temple. It is a type of prayer that provides solution to situations and brings direction in the face of challenges. This is the type of prayer Elijah prayed and for 3 ½ years, there was no rain in the land and he prayed again and heavy rain fall just at the instance of his prayer. The power available when we are effective in prayer is so much that it could create new things. There is tremendous power available when we pray effectively and that is what the Father wants us to have and operate here on earth.

COMPONENTS OF AN EFFECTIVE PRAYER

1. **It must be earnest**: The word earnest means serious and solemn. Serious in the manner and attitude of which it is made. Prayer is a serious business and demands seriousness if one take it for a joke or just an activity people do so you will not be seen an a pagan, then you are wrong. It is a serious activity that we must attach so much importance to. Prayer being solemn means it must be done in reverence when you speak the words of prayer, you must understand that you are speaking to the king of kings. Though the Holy Spirit intercedes for us before the Father, we must still pray in reverence knowing that He to whom we pray is a consuming fire. He is above all and creator of us all. There must be reverence in your prayer, it must be serious not a time of joke, you must show respect to God whom you are praying to; but in words and in your actions also.

2. **It must be heartfelt**: It must come from your heart arising from a strong and sincere emotion. Your prayer is supposed to be an expression of your heart to your Father. This is one component you cannot get from prayer books: God does not want you to read your desire; he wants us to express it from our heart. Your prayer has to come from the heart having your emotions expressed with it. Reading prayer books has never been how God want you to communicate with him. Can you imagine trying to have a conversation with your Father and all you are saying to him are things a third person wrote in a book and gave you, how then will your hearts connect one with another? Learn to pray to God on your own and express yourself in your best possible way.

   One day I was in a car with one of my colleagues, we started talking and he was so critical about the Pentecostal mode of prayer. He asked me a question; how can you come to your Father to ask him for something and you are shouting at him? I tried to help him understand that in prayer, God loves us to express our emotions. It is a heartfelt prayer, prayer coming from the heart and having with it all the feeling and emotions of your heart. It has to be a sincere expression of your heart to God in prayer. If the situation at the time of prayer stirred tears in your eyes, there is nothing wrong in expressing those while you pray even the Lord wept at the tomb of Lazarus while he was going to raise him up.

   Let us look at the prayer of king Hezekiah after the prophet Isaiah told the king that he would die from his sickness so that he should put his house in order 2king20:2-3

   Hezekiah turned his face to the wall. He prayed to the Lord and said "Lord remember that I have truly served you with all my heart. I have done the things that you said are good" then Hezekiah cried very hard.

   This prayer was a very brief but effective prayer that obtained an additional 15years for a man whom God was ready to call back home. The prophet Isaiah was not guessing the message he gave the king, God sent him with it. Yet when Hezekiah was pray from his heart, he touched the heart of God that the same prophet was sent again to declare an extension to Hezekiah's life. Looking at the words of this prayer it was not as though God forgot all that Hezekiah did as he said in his prayer for God does not forget, but the manner he made his appeal to God and the expression of his heart was what moved God to answer and heal him. If we want to be effective in our prayer it must be heartfelt.

3. **It has to be continuous**: this is one component that unlocks the power of prayer. Your ability to stay on a prayer until you sees what your desire is. This is not to say continue to pray a prayer point until you see it manifest, that is not what it means. A continued prayer means after you have finish saying the word of prayer, you position your actions and emotion and everything to get nothing else but the answer of what you prayed for. You wait in expectation not in doubt or unbelief. It means you pray and set your expectation on the answer you prayed for nothing else

Now you must believe your prayer- you must be fully persuaded that God is able to do what you are asking him to do for you and that He is willing to do that for you. Many times people pray and do not believe that what they are asking is possible. You have already slaughtered the prayer with doubt. You must believe God that He can do what you ask of Him and that He is going to do it for you because He loves you.

How this unlocks the power of prayer can be likened to a dynamo. A small device put on bicycle to generate power for the lamp at night. When a rider is pedaling continuously there is some power generated that the lamp will glow so bright, but if he pedals and stops and again, it will bring in the power and the glow will soon be over taken by darkness. Now when you pray and sustain your prayer by your expectation. It is like a rider on a bicycle that had dynamo, continues pedaling generating so much power that the lamp glows so bright. So when you pray, be earnest and pray from your heart but above all, never stop until you see what you have asked, continue to wait in expectation. The Lord Jesus said if you do not doubt but believe that what you said will happen; you will have whatsoever you said. There is tremendous power available when we pray and stay on our prayer. When we have faith that what we have asked, God is more than able to do and will do it for us, unspeakable power is available.

Prayer is a potent weapon God has given His children but as dangerous as machine gun is, if you do not know how to operate it, your enemy will still defeat you with clubs while you are battling him with a machine gun. The power available in the place of prayer can unlock any door and solve any situation in life. The power generated in the place of prayer can accomplish anything when we learn how to channel it properly. It is an earnest heartfelt continued prayer of the righteous that unlock the power for tremendous miracle.

PRAYING IN THE HOLY GHOST

Praying in unknown tongues and praying in the Holy Ghost is the same thing. It is a very important component of an effective prayer life. However, a lot of people find it confusing to pray in unknown tongue. When we pray in unknown tongue, you're giving the Holy Spirit full right to intercede for you before the Father. The scripture say we do not know what we ought to pray, yet when we pray, the Holy Spirit puts our prayer right and presents it to the Father. It is that request we are making that He presents before the Father but in a more appropriate way of expression. But when we pray in unknown tongue, the Holy Spirit is interceding for us of his own will. We have yielded to the Spirit to pray through us and you pray for things you do not even know which is not hidden from the Spirit of God.
Hence when pray in tongues we give the Holy Spirit opportunity to intercede for us according to the will of God. Many times we do not know what God will for us is and we just pray and say, "Lord let your will be done". This we can do better by praying in unknown tongue, for then the Holy Spirit who knows

what the mind of the Father is for us concerning that situation to makes intercession for us. When we pray in unknown tongue, we exercise our faith in God, believing that the Holy Spirit who knows the mind of God is interceding for us before the Father. The easiest way to get result in prayer is by asking in line with the will of God; and when the Holy Spirit interceding for us, it is according to the will of God. This is why praying in unknown tongue is such a powerful tool in prayer. Many people just pray in understanding and they do not pray in the spirit, we need a perfect blend of the two in our effective prayer walk.

For if I pray in an unknown tongue, my sprint pray but my understanding is unfruitful. What is it then? I pray with the spirit and I will pray with my understanding also. 1cor 14:14-15 KJV

For your prayer life to be effective and produce result you need to learn how to make a blend of praying in unknown tongue and praying in understanding. It is even much effective to pray in the spirit much more than in understanding so if all you do is praying in understanding alone, you are missing out a very wonderful component of your prayer. When you come to the place of prayer it is more effective to begin by praying in the Spirit. When we start our prayer by praying in unknown tongue, you stir the river of living water within until it overflows. When we stir the river within to overflow it flows into any situation of life we find ourselves in and makes it whole. In Ezek 47:1-14 the river that flows from the temple threshold (you are that temple) grew from level to level. It went from ankle level, to the knee level, to the waist level then to the level that you cannot walk in it, but swim it. This is the level that praying in understanding becomes very effective and productive. At this level, you do not ask, you speak things into being, at this level anything the river touched lived and was made whole and healing flowed with it. This is what happens when we pray in unknown tongue, stirring the river of living water till it overflow and then you begin to speak to that situation and challenge and circumstance. Praying in the Holy Ghost is a very important component of an effective prayer that we cannot overlook.

BENEFITS OF PRAYING IN THE SPIRIT

1. Praying in the spirit builds up your spiritual capacity:

A person who speaks in tongues is strengthened personally in the lord..." I Cor. 14:4

Praying in tongues is a way of increasing your spiritual muscle or strength. It is a spiritual exercise which builds up the spirit man to makes us strong and capable of receiving what God has prepared for us. Your dominion in life depends on your strength and your strength is increased as you pray in unknown tongue. The level of your spiritual exploit in your environment depends on your spiritual capacity. God relates with us based on our capacity in the spirit. The level of knowledge and revelation of God you can receive depends on your spiritual capacity. Every child of God has spiritual capacity and that determines the situations you can interfere with in the spirit. Pastor Tunde Bakare will say it takes a prince to bind a prince, but we are all having the same spirit. The difference is the capacity in the spirit.

In the physical, when a man want a man wants to acquire physical capacity or statue (muscle) he does exercise daily and his muscle capacity will increase to carry what he could not carry before. In the spirit if a child of God wants to gain spiritual capacity, He must learn to pray in the spirit.

But you, Beloved, build yourselves up (founded) on your most holy faith (make progress, rise like an edifice higher and higher}, praying in the Holy spirit Jude 1:20 AMP

If you want to rise higher and higher in stature, you can only achieve this by praying in the Holy Spirit. God wants sons on the earth who will daily put demons to flight like Jesus did when he walked the earth. For you to acquire such capacity, you need to be praying in the Holy Spirit. The things you can resist in the spirit depends on your spiritual capacity, If you have a muscle like a baby, every situation will just come and overtake you, but if you have the statue of sons, you can stand and resist.

Every situation comes to try your muscle, anyone that over powers you keep you down, but if your spiritual muscle is developed, you can press it down and remain on top of it.

When we pray in unknown tongue, we increase our spiritual capacity to unveil the Glory of God. Glory has weight and the level of Glory you can manifest depends on your capacity in the spirit. If your spiritual muscle cannot carry 50kg weight of Glory, no matter how you can ask God for it, God will never manifest such through you. It is as you exercise to increase your spiritual capacity that you enable yourself to receive more of what God has in plan for you.

The power of God is beyond limit but the level of it you can manifest in your life time depends on your spiritual capacity. If we want to rise up like an edifice higher and higher, if you desire men to see the Glory of God in your life like never before, then you need an increased spiritual capacity, you need to pray in the Holy Ghost.

2. Praying in the spirit Brings insight to the word of God.

"That is what is meant by the scriptures which say that no mere man has ever seen, heard or even imagined what wonderful this God has ready for those who love the lord. But we know about these because God has sent his spirit to tell us and his spirit searches out and show us all of God's deepest secrets." 1 Cor. 2: 9-10 (TLB)

This is what happens when we pray in the Holy Ghost. It is when we pray in unknown tongue that the Holy Spirit opens our eyes to these deep secrets of God. Praying in the spirit gives us access to seeing things that no eyes has ever seen, and to hear things no ear has ever heard, things that the mind can never conceive. When we pray in unknown tongue, the Holy Ghost who searches the mind of God, shows us even Gods deep secrets. Moses was drawn by the spirit of God to the mountain and tarried and by God's spirit, he was given access to see events of creation by God. He even saw the tabernacle in heaven.

The word of God is God's own way of expressing the things he has in mind for His people. No man can know what the mind of God is or what God thought really is

"No one really knows what anyone else is thinking or what he is really like except that person himself and no one can know God's thought except God's own spirit" 1 Cor. 2:11 TLB

The bible is God's thought or dream book to his people, it contains in it the mind of God for his children here on earth. Yet no one can really understand it except by the help of God's spirit. God has given us his spirit for this purpose so we can know the wonderful things he has freely given to us when we learn to stir the spirit. The depth of revelation of the word of God you see depends on the depth of your stirring of the spirit of God in the place of prayer. When you pray in the spirit before you study your bible, you open the eyes of your spirit man for greater insight. Remember it is God's glory to conceal a thing; God hides deeper benefits of his word for deep searchers.

3. Praying in the Holy Ghost lends power to your words.

Praying in the spirit is a way of allowing the great intercessor to intercede for you before the Father. When you pray in tongues and focus on God, after a while direction and utterance comes. God puts his word in your mouth concerning your situation and so you speak it, it produces the same impact as when God himself has spoken. It opens the connection between man and God and gives man privilege to speak like God. Praying in the spirit makes you speak in God's language. God puts the appropriate word for the moment in your heart and as you speak it, it opens the door and brings result. The same way creation cannot disobey the voice of God, that situation will hearken to your command.

4. Praying in the spirit makes it easy for you to hear the voice of God.

There are times when all things don't seem to make sense. You find yourself confused and stranded. May be you need a direction out of a pressing predicament. That is not a time to cry or call people for counsel; it is rather a time to consult the counselor within. This happens also by praying in the Holy Ghost. When we pray in the spirit, you shut the door of flesh and focus on the Holy Ghost. He will release the direction of what to do to get out of that situation. This can be seen in the life of Moses, in front of the Red sea with the Egyptians behind him and the people with him blaming him and mountains on both sides of him. It could not get worse than that, but the scripture said he prayed. Praying in the Holy Ghost is the easiest way to communicate with God in such times to get direction.

Praying in the spirit silences the flesh and makes your thought and intellect unnecessary as you focus all your attention on God. This is why it is very easy to get direction and hear God when you pray in the Holy Ghost. Praying in the Spirit blanks out your mind of thoughts and makes it easy for God to drop words in your spirit. It is like robbing off everything on a white board for God to write his will on it. This is what we achieve when we pray in tongues. It makes it easy for us to hear God and get direction in the face of confusion. Anytime you need direction from God or find yourself in a tight state of confusion, the only thing to do is to seek God's way out and you will always get direction when you take time to pray in the Holy Ghost.

5) Praying in unknown tongue opens all locked gates in the path of life and destiny.

Gates are boundaries of limitation set to limit ones movement in a particular direction. It is a stronghold set to hinder progress. If you have even witnessed where gates are set up, you will see how strong their pillars are made and heavy so that you cannot just push them down to walk over. In the path of Destiny, there are gates. They come to limit you so that you will cross to the other side. Some of them look so strong as if nothing on earth can pull them down. Many people when they get to such gate end their journey and set camps and remain there. But God is a gate breaker. When we are faced with gates so strong, so impenetrable, that should tell you that there is only one person who can open this gate and that is God. Whenever God shows up, gates open on their accord; whenever the people of God pray in the spirit, gates unlock on their own also. It is just like Paul and Silas praying in prison and gates opening on their own accord. They just brought down the presence of the God whom no gates can limit and the gates opened on its accord. When you pray in the Spirit, you stir up the river of living water within. When the Holy Ghost arises through you the gates will open. When you face gates of limitation on the path of your Destiny, do not make camp there, pray in the spirit and the power of God will unlock the gates for you to pass through.

Praying in the Spirit must be a very important part of our prayer walk as Christians. The Holy Spirit who is the great intercessor should not be kept mute, let us give him opportunity to intercede for us before the Father. It is only when we learn to give the Holy Spirit his place in our prayer life that we will always obtain result at the end of the day.

CHAPTER 6

THE BELIEVER'S LIFESTYLE OF FAITH.

"Now the just shall live by faith: but if any man drawback, my soul shall have no pleasure in him". Heb 10:38

Everyone who has been called in Christ Jesus to walk with God must learn to operate by faith. Faith is the life sustaining force of the new creation man. In the natural realm of life, man depends on oxygen to live, if you can take oxygen away from natural life, it ceases as the creature dies be it man or beast. In the Spiritual, we are called to live by faith, relate with God by faith as the only life line available to the recreated man. There is no substitute for faith in your walk with God. No man can ever bring pleasure to God without living by faith. In fact, the scripture acknowledge one impossibility for the recreated man – it is impossible to please God without faith. Heb 11:6.

If we are called in Christ Jesus to follow the footsteps of Christ, then we will understand that our major call is to please God with our lives. The Lord Jesus pleases the Father always during the time of his earthly ministry. At a point in the scripture he declared that the Father has not left him alone because he always does those things that pleased him. As a child of God, washed by the blood of sacrifice, you cannot attain any level in God if your life can not please the Father. Our faith is the only instrument we have to please God, the only equipment we use to bring pleasure to the Father. Many people have seen faith to be equipment we use to collect things from God something we deploy when we have needs from God but the primary purpose of faith is to please God rather than collecting things from him.

WHAT IS FAITH?

Faith is to believe what God says is, is and what He says will be will be.

The central thought in faith is God, and his word, to be fully persuaded of the existence of God even in our subconscious and relating with this persuasion.

Abraham is called the Father of faith and his faith brought righteousness to him. (Gen 15:6) What Abraham did was to believe in the Lord; he was convinced of the person of God. He was persuaded of God; he accepted, acknowledged and recognized the existence of God. A lot of people just acknowledge the existence of God but do not recognize him or regard him. Abraham is the Father of faith because he acknowledged and recognized God. He believed in the Lord; - He recognized that there is someone who owns and has control over everything that happens to him; he recognized that he was not the one in charge. When we understand that we are not the ones that run things but Jehovah, it becomes easy to relate with this word and do its demand. When Abraham recognized the personality of God as the one in charge, he also believed what God says to him and acted in the direction of what God says to him. God does not have an opinion in many people's life today yet they claim that they know him or believe in him. The proof that you recognize the personality of God is seen by how much of his word you adhere to. For you to believe what God says – you must first know who God is and be persuaded that God is. The scripture say that he that will come to God must first believe that he – God exist". You must be fully persuaded of that to the point that you can believe his words. You cannot believe the words of a God you do not believe exist.

The next thing that faith tells apart from the existence of God is his integrity. Faith talks about relating with the integrity of God – it is believing what God said is, is and what he said will be, will be.

Whenever you doubt God, you do not doubt his existence as a child of God, but you doubt his integrity. Has he said, will he do it? A man of faith is one who believes the integrity and infallibility of the word of God. A lot of people don't count the word of God for anything even though they acknowledge that God is. Such people cannot operate by faith and such life cannot please God. You must believe in the integrity of God and the infallibility of his word to be a man of faith. In fact Abraham won righteousness not just by doing all things right but just believing in the infallibility of the word of God and God rewarded him with righteousness. Your believe in the integrity of God and the infallibility of his word is so precious to Him that he can give you the whole world as a reward for doing that. When we have a problem with any of these two things, we will find it difficult to operate by faith. When people cannot see the integrity of God and his word, they cannot trust him and such people cannot walk by faith towards God. Faith is seeing God as God and relating with him as such. God is the Supreme Being that created all things and governs the creation by his word and power. He is all powerful and all capable and can do all things. There is absolutely nothing outside the jurisdiction of his power. When we see our God in the real definition of who he is and relate with him in same light that is faith.

HOW CAN I PLEASE GOD WITH MY FAITH?

The primary purpose of faith is to please God and this is how my faith pleases God; when we have come to acknowledge and recognize the personality of God in our lives and consciously adhere to the instructions of his word that brings pleasure to God. When we regard God in our lives and we follow his word, we bring pleasure to him.

There is nothing that pleases the Father like his people seeing him for who he is and relating with him in like manner.

Faith is seeing God as God and relating with him alike. When we see God as God and not man and we relate to his words as the word of God not the words of man, this is faith and this pleases the Father. It is unfortunate that many people see God as many other things except as God, hence we place undue limitations on him and his word. Some people in abiding to see God as their Father unconsciously transfer the limitations of their earthly Fathers and other limitations of man and place it on God; hence they cannot please God by our faith – which is to see God as God and relate with him and his word as the word of God. The word "God" is the best the human language could come up with to refer to a supreme being, if there was any other word greater than God that is what Jehovah really is. However, let us just stay with this word God. It means the Supreme Being that is almighty and all powerful. The first lesson of faith is that God is Almighty. No wonder when God appeared to Abraham, he introduced himself as God Almighty – walk before me and be perfect. For you to have faith that produces result especially such that pleases the Father, you must first come to the point of realization that this God is the Almighty. The greatest and most powerful. The essence of all existence and the only potent force in the entire universe. This was the reason God did not introduce himself to Abraham as a provider – which he later did; He first called himself as Almighty God. Have you known him as Almighty? Or do you still think he is mighty but not all mighty? The office of almightiness of God means he can do absolutely anything and all things. This was the lesson Abraham learnt and it was easy to believe God and God accounted it to him as righteousness.

After we have confirmed it to our hearts that God is Almighty, we need to also understand that he is Jehovah – the one who brings substance to his words. This was the next level God revealed to Moses. He told him that, to Abraham he revealed himself as God almighty but by his name Jehovah was He not known to them at that time. If your faith will obtain and bring pleasure to the Father, you must first know God as Almighty and Jehovah. These two revelations are the foundations of the faith that will please God. God is a Spirit and dwells in the realms of the Spirits, but he gave us his word and his Spirit by which he still speaks to us today. If anyone will not take the word of God as the word of a mere man, he must first understand that God is Almighty and that he fulfils his word without anything stopping him.

The greatest problem of man in relation to our walk of faith is how we see God. Some people see God as one of the gods of their land that will always disappoint at the time of need, like Baal to the prophets of Baal. Others see God as man who created the world and lives in heaven such that sometimes situations get out of his control and he frets. All these perceptions of God are faulty and will never allow the person who have them build faith in this Almighty Creator.

"Because that, when they knew God, they glorified him not on God, neither were they thankful; but became vain in their imaginations as their foolish heart was darkened... and changed the glory of the incorruptible God into an image made like to corruptible man, and to birds and four footed beasts and creeping things". Romans 1: 21 &23

The scripture talked about man who knew God- (a supreme being who is over all and under none, who is supreme over all things) but they glorified him not as God. They could have acknowledged him as powerful, but not all powerful. They could have acknowledged him as Supreme Being, but not supreme over all things. They still put some limitations on God. They did not glorify him as God. These people being referred to in this scripture are in the church today, believers, they believe that God is powerful far more powerful than man but can he furnish a table in the wilderness? Can he raise the dead back to life?

Another category this scripture referred to was those who made God. These people cannot bear the fact that God is the essence of all things, never created creator, hence they recreated God in their hearts in the image of fallen man, and birds and beast of the earth (no matter how powerful the beast is) and creeping things. So these people recreate a perfect God into an imperfect being, who can acts in the ways of imperfect man or beast. So like man when you offend God, he will consume you with his anger just like how these people will destroy anyone who displeases them if they had the power; yet God has not consumed these people because He takes no pleasure in the death of the wicked. The scriptures clearly states that God is not a man and his ways are higher than the ways of man because his thoughts are higher than our thoughts. So instead of trying to recreate God in your own image understand that God is not a man neither does he operate in the ways of man.

How do you see God? Do you see him like man or like the Lion that is the King of the jungle but only a beast and can be tamed, or do you see him as the Almighty whose words hold immerse power?. Faith is to see God as God and to relate with his words as the word of God. If your faith will please God, you must first understand that he is almighty and that his words are the words of the Almighty God not just the rant of a man and believe it. When you see God as God and relate to his word as the word of God you please God. This is how we please the Father by faith. Do not see God as any other thing but for who he is and relate with him and his word as the word of the Almighty, the final authority. When we live like this we please God.

Obedience is a fruit of faith; when we operate by faith we will find it easy to obey God's instructions and this will deliver us from destruction and bring peace to us and gladness and these are God's desire towards his children.

BELIEVERS WALK OF FAITH

God said to Abraham to leave his Father's house and his kindred to a land that he will show him and Abraham left all the known to follow the unknown. This is faith. Faith will make you build your life on the unknown and uncertain while others will like to build on fact and reality. The difference is that faith brings the impossible into reality. A man of faith creates new realities in history, but if you live your life on facts, you can only live in the history another person has created.

The lifestyle of faith is calling for all who have come to Christ. It is the only pattern of life acceptable in the beloved where we have been translated. Abraham was a reality maker, so also was Isaac, Jacob and everyone who ever walked with God by faith. Our walk of faith is what gives us the privilege of creating new things in our world. A faithless generation will not create new realities and will find it difficult to even believe the testimonies of people who had walked in these realities in the past. Faith gives us access to operating in the realm of God's power. What are you creating with this privilege?

Abraham by faith became the Father of many nations and is called the friend of God. Moses by faith parted the sea floor. Gideon by faith used 300 men to conquer an army of trained warriors; David by faith used a stone to kill a giant who defiled the name and army of his God etc. These are realities that men created in the past by faith; what are you doing with your faith? Sadly, in the church today, we use faith to build large church auditoriums, buy private jets and win contracts; and God is expecting much more. As good as these things are, they are the elementary things we should invest our precious privilege with God and do. This generation is dying for new realities aside from the ones written in scriptures, God is so eager to show the world new marvels than what we have read in bible but where are the believer that he will use to showcase these things?

There is so much in God that if we launch our faith into the deep, we will bring deep things that will change the course of the generation. The preaching of the gospel of God's kingdom is not just a mere talk, it is a power demonstration. The 21st century is dying to see reality created that science cannot explain. What are you doing with your faith?

If only we can begin to walk in faith, our lives will create new realities every other days. When the Lord walked the earth, he was not seeking to create realities for his generation; he just lived and his daily life became a wonder till this day. Let us rise on the wings of faith today and transform this generation by the wonders of our faith until they cannot understand it anymore. It is only by faith can we bring the terror and the awe of our God back to this generation. Our calling to walk by faith is not just for you to collect materials from heaven; faith is not just a device to meet our needs on earth that is the lowest application of faith. Faith is your tool to reign on the earth and amaze the world for our God. Faith is for us to please the Father always like the Lord himself did.

CHAPTER 7

THE SECRET CALLED KNOWLEDGE

According as his divine power hath given unto us all things that pertain to life and godliness, through the knowledge of him that hath called us to glory and virtue... 2Pet 1:3

There is a place where you can have all things that life and godly living requires on this planet and this place has been made available to us the new creation but is only accessible through the knowledge of him that has called us. In the kingdom were we live now, knowledge is a currency that you can use to obtain the things that has been made available for you. Over and over again in scriptures God has always invested in teaching his children knowledge because this is the only key that will position them for kingdom exploits. When Jesus walked the earth he invested three and half years of his life in ministry teaching the knowledge of the kingdom. When the Holy Spirit was promised by the Lord one of the major things He will do in us was to teach us all things and reveal the knowledge of the kingdom to us. So time and time again God still keep reaching out to us to teach us the secret of knowledge because this is one weapon the enemy is using to deceive the people and destroy them.

My people are destroyed for lack of knowledge: because thou hast rejected knowledge, I will also reject thee, that thou shalt be no priest to me: seeing thou hast forgotten the law of thy God, I will also forget thy children. Hosea 4:6

This prophesy of Hosea stands true to all generations even as far back as the time of Adam and Eve in Eden. The fall of man in the garden and the destruction of the empire that God built for the man he loved called Eden was all a product of lack of knowledge which we will call ignorance. Had it been that the man God put in the garden in the comfort of all that the Father by himself has made available had known that his creation was in the image of God and after God's likeness (in operation) so that we were already like him ruling in a sphere or domain of the physical just as Jehovah rules in the unseen worlds, had man had this knowledge he would not have fallen to the lies of Satan. The lie that you will be like God only after you have eaten the fruit of the tree of knowledge of good and evil would have been a walkover for man had he known he was already the god in his realm.

Many of us pray today and do not get answers from heaven because we are so ignorant about God and the things he would have us know and our ignorance limits our prayer before God. Infact God said he will reject those that reject knowledge and they will not have a place in him. Stop looking away from knowledge so that you will not be rejected. One of the things that make the realm of the recreated man better than Eden is the fact that ignorance does not live there. Infact what admits you to this kingdom of Christ is knowledge, the knowledge that Christ has come in the flesh and paid the penalty for your sins and made a way for you to come back home. Except this knowledge hit you, like the prodigal son you will still be comfortable sharing meals with pigs and sleeping with them.

Your place in Christ Jesus is a place where knowledge is a currency and when you are devoid of it, you cannot transact with God here on earth. In the physical realm when a man is devoid of money in any of its currencies, he is poor, stranded and helpless and cannot obtain anything no matter how he so desires and cries for that because there is a way that has been made through which you can obtain anything whatsoever you desire; once you have the money to purchase that, it is yours fully. So also is this true in Christ Jesus, when anyone is devoid of knowledge which is the currency used in the realm of the recreated man, he is powerless and helpless and cannot obtain anything no matter how hard he seeks that in prayer. Prayer is good and very important but is never the master key like we have been taught. Prayer cannot obtain for you what you are supposed to get through knowledge no matter how hard you pray it with fasting. Cornelius in the bible was a devote man and sincere in his pursuit of salvation and prayed often but the best his prayer could do was to bring an angelic encounter to point him in the right direction which was to seek out Peter who had the knowledge of what he was to do to be saved. All his prayers and arms could not save him because it was not the job of prayer to save him but knowledge. There is a way that has been made through which you can obtain anything in the kingdom of Christ and until you follow it you cannot obtain anything in Christ. The knowledge of Christ is the way to obtain, not just the factual knowledge of his existence but the applied knowledge that brings experience and skill. People in a community speak same language and have same culture which is people's way of doing things, in Christ Jesus we must grow in knowledge of him till we come to the place where we speak the same language (not talking about your tongues) and have same culture regardless of our geographical location on earth because we are all located in Christ Jesus in the spirit.

God has given to us all that we need for life and godliness but only accessible through knowledge. We are living in the age where your faith will not be enough; you will require adding to your faith, knowledge for it to obtain for you. A lot of people do not understand the difference in the times that we are in and upgrade to what is necessary hence they still hold on to their faith after all the just shall live by his own faith but they do not know that it is through knowledge the righteous shall be delivered. Faith never stands alone; infact faith helps you to find knowledge. The scriptures said by faith we understand that the worlds were framed by the word of God. In the kingdom of Christ knowledge is our currency and the more of it you have the more you will be able to live the full life that Christ has bought for us.

WHAT THEN IS KNOWLEDGE

According to dictionary definition, knowledge is facts, information and skills acquired through experience or education. It is also the practical understanding of a subject. There are 3 levels of knowledge:

Factual Knowledge: it's just an accumulation of facts or information about things but having no relationship with the facts or information. This is just awareness of facts without necessarily taking the facts to accounts in your actions and inactions. Most people believe there is God somewhere but that knowledge will not affect how they live or relate with their neighbors neither will they acknowledge him in their daily living. When you operate in this level of knowledge the best you can be is a religious folk with a lot of fact about life but unable to relate with any of them in a way that imparts your life.

Understanding: this level of knowledge imparts the life of him that walk in it as he begins to operate in line with the fact or information he has and begins to pattern his life in line with these facts. This is the level of knowledge that leads people to new birth when you understand that God so loved you and you have been running away from him and living in a way that will destroy your soul, so you repent and change your ways.

Wisdom is the principle thing; therefore get wisdom. And in all your getting get understanding. Prov 4:7

Understanding is a profitable level of knowledge that imparts the life of the person that has it. When you gain understanding of healthy living you will begin to avoid certain food that will affect your health which you would have ordinarily eaten. Until the knowledge you claim to have changes the way you do things, you do not have understanding. When you operate in this level of knowledge you will obtain favour and make your way easy. Prov 13:15

Wisdom: This level of knowledge not only imparts your life but also affects your judgement and your manner of living. It is the level where the information you have is not just a mere fact but has been proven by experience and has become a skill or principle. This is the level of knowledge John was talking about in 1John 1:1, he said the things we heard (information), our eyes have seen and our hands have handled (experience). So at this level you turn information to experience. This is the level of knowledge that rewards anyone that has it not just with favour but puts you in the exact place of authority God has always wanted you and I to operate from.

So shall the knowledge of wisdom be unto thy soul: when thou hast found it, then there shall be a reward and thy expectation shall not be cut off. Prov 24:14

This level of knowledge is not operated by many people, it's a hidden knowledge and there is evidence that follows anyone who is able to operate at this level. The first thing is that there will be a reward which may come in form of prosperity or honour. The second thing that happens to anyone who operates this level of knowledge is that your expectations will not be cut off. At this point you can speak a thing and it will come to pass not because you quoted scripture or prayed but because there is an end that must line up to your expectation.

I have always loved the story of Elijah in the bible that went before a king and said to him as the Lord lives there will be neither dew nor rain in the next few years except at my word. I have always wondered the secret of Elijah's boldness to make such a demand that there should be no rain or dew but at his word. He was not just walking in faith, Elijah operated in this level of knowledge where you can speak a thing and it will come to pass. When you attain this level of knowledge concerning anything in life even business, you will without fail obtain the reward and authority that follows it.

The knowledge we are talking of is the knowledge of Christ (him that has called us). So when you upgrade your knowledge of God from just a mere story of things that happened many years ago, to understanding the scriptures as God's word to his children and you live by them and make them the principles of your existence and harken diligently to do all it teaches you will get to this level of operation of knowledge called wisdom where you will have reward and authority. How much of Christ have you known and become, when we behold him(Christ) as a mirror learning about him and following in his ways we will become transformed from glory to glory till we are perfected in his image again. This is what knowledge does for us in Christ Jesus, it makes us become like our master and only then can we manifest as the sons of God.

It is the goal of the Father that everyone who has been translated into the kingdom of Christ should look like Jesus, operate the same way he operated and depend on the Father the same way he did while he walked the earth. There is no one else that meets the perfect image of the son that pleases the Father except Jesus Christ, and that is the only image we are called to be like not like your pastor or any other man of God whatsoever. Have you ever wondered why Judas had to use a kiss to show the chief priest and his mob the person that was the master on the night Jesus was arrested in Gethsemane? In all the four gospels, the chief priest and his team that came to arrest the Lord needed someone to show them the person that was Jesus on the night of the arrest lest they arrest the wrong person. Why? Could it be that they all looked alike? Or maybe they wore same cloth and had same appearance that it was needed that someone from inside to give the Lord away? John told us that the things they heard as factual knowledge while following the master later became experiential knowledge for them (our hands have handled) concerning the knowledge of him that has called us, hence they already became like the Lord so that you cannot say for sure who among the community of disciples was Jesus. No wonder Judas got so much money that could buy a land to just point to the one that was the Lord. The community we are called to be in Christ is supposed to be like this, where everyone looks like the master and Christ is in all working through all.

Now that you are born again, don't just remain in religion, but understand what the Father desires of you and do it. Your Job is not to be tied to a denomination and serve a man of God but to grow in grace and knowledge of him that have called us till you come to the fullness of his stature and like him live out the culture of kingdom of Christ. Eph 4:12 talks about the work and purpose of the church on earth as the tool for equipping the saints for the work of the ministry, training by application of knowledge the believers till we all come to unity of faith and knowledge of God. The unity means having same level of faith and applicable knowledge of God so that the believer who is in Christ Jesus can operated like Jesus who is our perfect example. This is the reason God gave the ministerial gift so that no one should feel special with God but fulfill their role in the kingdom of Christ. Whether you are an Apostle, a Prophet, Evangelist, Pastor or Teacher your job is to help the saints come to the same level of faith and knowledge of Christ that you have, grooming them to walk in the experiential knowledge of God and his word by being an example for them till we all become like Jesus walking in the culture of the kingdom with ease. Your job is not to privatize God so that you now look special with God and they are not, so until I say the God of Francis Okenwa, he will not answer. In the Old Testament God appeared to Jacob in bethel as the God of Abraham and Isaac his Father just as a way of giving Jacob a reference point and so he won't see God as a strange God, but the God of his Father that he had not known. There is no perfect son anywhere aside Jesus and if anyone has the right to privatize God its Christ but he calls him our God. In fact in all scriptures Paul was the only one who referred to God in such manner.

Blessed be the God and Father of our Lord Jesus Christ, who has blessed us with all spiritual blessings in heavenly places in Christ: Eph1:3

Let no one deceive you to think of them as highly placed in Christ because we are all the same and all washed by the precious blood of Jesus and all loved by the Father. There is only knowledge gap in the kingdom and if you will give yourself to finding the knowledge of him that has called us, you will also become a mature son in the kingdom.

CHAPTER 8

CHRIST OUR DWELLING PLACE

"For in him we live, and move and have our being..." Act 17: 28a

Just as it was at the beginning when God created man, he placed him in a garden – a realm called Eden from where he was to rule the earth and all creatures and subdue them. As long as man operated from Eden, he ruled the earth and creation was absolutely subject to him. Until after the fall of man and God sent man out of the garden to operate in the realm of earth. This same pattern that we see in creation of man is same pattern that exists in the recreation of man. At the death and resurrection of Christ, a redemption program for mankind was initiated, this program was to restore man to operate in the same way he was created to; live on the earth and operate from a realm above the earth.

However, the only difference is that this time, the redeemed man was not sent back to Eden as it was at the beginning, rather a better place, far better than Eden was prepared for man. The scripture calls it the kingdom of God's dear son.

"Who hath delivered us from the power of darkness and hath translated us into the kingdom of his dear son". Col 1:13

As perfect and beautiful as Eden was, there was a problem with it; it was accessible to Satan. No wonder the serpent could creep in and deceive the woman. Also God himself was not resident in Eden; he comes at the cool of the evening from his own dwelling place to fellowship with man in Eden and what a wonderful fellowship it was. Man could hear God speak word for word with him and respond and live. It was indeed a good place except for these two issues, the devil had access to Eden and God was not a permanent resident of Eden. He was a visitor who only came during visiting time and go afterwards; - this was the greatest loophole of Eden.

However, after the redemptive work of Christ, the Father prepared a better place for us. Like the scripture we quoted above, "the kingdom of God's dear son" is the dwelling place of the redeemed man. It is not the place we will go when we die or at the catching away of the saints, no! It is the place where you and I are supposed to operate from while still on earth, just as it was in the beginning.

When you become born again; you have accepted Christ as your Lord and Saviour and been baptized into him, you are immediately translated to this kingdom of God's dear son. This place can also be referred to as "in Christ". Christ is a place and that is where we live and move and have our being. It is such a glorious place to be and a few things we will highlight about this place called "Christ Jesus"

Firstly, its location is far above principality and power in the heavenly places. The scriptures made this clear in the verse below –

"And God raised us up with Christ and seated us with him in the heavenly realms in Christ Jesus. Eph 2:6 (NIV)

We are seated together with Christ in the heavenly realm in Christ Jesus and the location of Christ Jesus is in the heavenly realm. It is not a physical location but a spiritual dimension from where we operate here on earth. Every one that has been born again is meant to live and operate from here and be free from

Satan's torments and wickedness of men. This is the first privilege that we enjoy in Christ Jesus; we are beyond the reach of Satan and his demons. If you are still being tormented by the devil, it can only mean you have not been born again hence you have not been translated. Going to church and being a Christian is not same as being a believer. For you to be a believer you must be born again but to a Christian you just need to be member of a congregation and pay your tithe and be early to church.

HOW HIGH ABOVE IS CHRIST JESUS (our dwelling place)?

Paul, in the book of Ephesians chapter one was praying for the church that their eyes of understanding be enlightened to know the hope of their calling and the riches of the glory of God's inheritance in his saints. And much more that they may know the exceeding greatness of God's power available to us who believe; according to the working of God's mighty power.

"which he wrought in Christ when he raised him from the dead and set him at his own right hand in heavenly places, far above all principalities and power and might and dominion and every name that is named, not only in this world but also in the world which is to come" Eph 1: 20 -21

God demonstrating the greatness of his power, raised Christ and set him up on the heavenly places – far above all principalities and powers and might and dominion and names, and we are seated together with Christ in this place. So the dwelling place of the recreated man is such that no demon or witches and wizards can attend there. Christ Jesus is a place far beyond the reach of Satan & his host and this is where we operate from. The scripture said it was set up as a demonstration of the greatness of God's power to us, hence it is only when Satan's power becomes far more than the power of God can we who have been translated to the kingdom of God's dear son become accessible to his operation and dominions and this can never happen. So our place of dwelling in God is way better than what we lost in Adam. Also this kingdom of God's dear son is at the right hand of the Father, the place where God's power is always at its peak. The plan of God is that we who live and move and have our being in Christ should reveal this greatness of his power to the world that has not known him. One more thing that is so exciting about this place we dwell is that the King walks in our midst. It is not like Eden that God was only a visitor, in Christ Jesus, God is a resident with us and the host of all the angels of God, hence there is no Satan or demon that can ever wander by chance into this realm, it is a realm of absolute protection. It is an amazing place to work from and just like in Eden, God speaks to us all the time, his voice is heard in our Spirit and speak back to him directly without any need for a prophet or an intermediary to stand before him for us. If you are a citizen of this realm, you cannot be a "my pastor say" believer, because you will drink from the same well your pastor drinks and hear God the same way your pastor hears him and speak to God the same way your Pastor speaks to him and he will answer you the same way he answers your pastor.

Christ Jesus is a beautiful place and a place of power. You can not dwell there in and be a fearful Christian, tormented by the devil, conquered by demons, afraid of witches and wizards.

HOW DO I TRULY BECOME TRANSLATED?

The word "translate" simply means to move something from one place to another. As it relates to our discussion, our translation was the movement of man's spirit from operating from the realms of earth to the realm of the kingdom of God's dear son. This movement is not a physical movement but spiritual and it is true. Once a man is born again and is baptized into Christ, he is translated to the realm of God's dear son. This kingdom of God's dear son in the Old Testament was referred to as "the secret place of the most high"

"He that dwelleth in the Secret place of the most high shall abide under the shadow of the Almighty" Psalm 91:1

The secret place of the most high is this place of abode of the recreated man, the kingdom of God's dear son. To dwell in this kingdom you have to be translated into it through the blood of the Lamb of God whose blood was shed for the forgiveness of sins of the whole world. When a man genuinely gives his life to Christ which happens by confessing to the finished works of Christ and putting your faith in the sacrifice of Christ to be reconciled to God, not in anything else that is the beginning of salvation. The part of being baptized into Christ which is usually symbolized by what baptism by immersion, talks about imbibing the doctrine of Christ and living it as your life principle. If you have confessed with your mouth but have not yielded your life to the doctrine of Christ, you are not really saved yet, you are at best admitted into religion and nothing happens at this point. You must confess with your mouth the Lord Jesus and believe in your heart that God raised him from the dead for you to be saved. To believe means to accept that something is true, especially without proof. Your belief is not just that God raised him from the dead but why did God raise him from the dead? God raised him for your justification and to be the first born among many brethren, if then brethren we must live the kind of life Christ came to show us here when we walked the earth.

Ps. 91:1 just puts it simple – *"abide under the shadow of the Almighty"*.

A shadow is a product of light cast on a non – transparent object, when a shadow is cast, the object controls its shape, movement and entire existence. If we abide under the shadow of the Almighty, it means the Almighty should control the way we think, the things we do, the place we go etc. we are supposed to be subject to the spirit of God just the same way the shadow is subject to the object that cast it. This is what baptism into Christ is really means. When I have been baptized into Christ, I have taken the teachings of Christ to become the principles of my existence not just a story we tell children in church and school. Until a man is born again and baptized into Christ, he is not translated into the kingdom of God's dear son and cannot begin to enjoy the benefits of Christ. This is not to say you must be perfect before you are translated, no! You must be born again and you must be baptized into him for you to be translated. You must have accepted the ways and opinions of Christ, his teaching and his requirements as the way to go and be fully convinced in your heart about this. We have in the past had where people confess they have been born again while they continue living the way they like, that is not true repentance. You must repent and forsake your old ways and be baptized into the doctrine of Christ to follow it every inch of the way. The apostle Paul was a Pharisee who persecuted the believers, but when we repented he did not continue in his old ways and religion of his Fathers, but he turn to the knowledge of Christ. If your repentance does not bring new life, it is not complete. One of the evidence of translation is that you will no longer be comfortable in your old ways, things that didn't matter before will begin to matter because your perspective have changed. If you were a fornicator and after you gave your life to Christ, you still do not see without an external compulsion, why you must leave fornication them, you didn't really accept the Lord. When you sincerely and truly accept the Lord as your savior and give up your old ways and embrace the way of the Lord, then you will be translated.

At his point, you may not have mastered victory over your habits, but you are no longer a slave to them. All you need is fellowship with God and his word and brethren to fully conquer and gain victory over the habits you were given to as a sinner. When you are a citizen of Christ Jesus, it does not mean you will never again face temptations and trials, it only means that sin will not have dominion over you anymore. It means when the opportunity to do evil present itself, you have a new nature that will say – "not for me, I will pass". There are many other privileges that abound in Christ Jesus and as we grow in grace & knowledge of the lord Jesus, we learn how to access these things and enjoy better life here on earth

CHAPTER 9

OUR DOMINION MANDATE IN CHRIST

"And God blessed them, and God said unto them, be fruitful, and multiply, and replenish the earth, and subdue it: and have dominion over the fish of the sea, and over the fowl of the air and over everything thing that moveth upon the earth". Gen 1:28

At the creation of man in the beginning as one of the creations of God, man was given a mandate. The dominion mandate given to man was to subdue creation and have dominion over all God's creations. By this mandate man related with all the beast of creation in the garden including lions and other dangerous creatures we have today on land and sea. The dominion mandate guaranteed man's supremacy over other creations and these creatures accorded man this respect without man demanding it. In fact God brought all the animals to man he gave them the names that we have today and we are still naming the ones we are just discovering till date. As far as man continued to operate in the realm of Eden, man enjoyed this dominion mandate which operated by default on other creations. However, when man fell by disobeying God and was sent out of Eden, we lost the dominion mandate. The mandate was reset in the beast of the earth, and birds of the air and the fish of the sea. This is because man was sent from a realm that is above the earth from where he operated to operate and live in the earthly realm just like these other creatures. Hence our intellect became the only base for dominion no longer by default like it was in Eden. This is why lions will see a man and see a food, same goes to sharks and other creatures of the sea like crocodiles etc. Even Bacteria that was suppose to work for man's good started killing man because man now has been brought to operate in the same realm as these creatures because of the fall.

When man was still in Eden, God brought the entire beasts he created to see what man will call them and probably if he could find a companion, a partner among them. The scriptures said man could not find a help – meet among these creatures which now made God to separate the female man from the male man so they can be companion to each other. But after man was sent out of Eden and sent to operate in the realm of earth like every other beast, man now sees dogs as a partner that some people get married to their dogs, cats and other pets. Men now sleep with animals to have sex with them and women also sleeping with animals like dogs etc. In the beginning it was not so. If it would have been, Adam had the chance to make the call, but he could not find any among all these creatures that man now sleep with and make their companions, he could not find any one a help meet for man. The reason was that man was operating from a higher realm and could not partner with another creature operating in the realm of earth; it was not long before man started finding pleasure in animals which was not meant to be.

Man so fell from grace to the point that there was no more dominion. Other creatures saw man like every other animal in the jungle and related with man in same manner. The dominion mandate was abolished and gone. Man had to use his intellect and civilization to keep off the other animals from attack and invasion. The elements of earth subjected man to its harsh conditions and killed and keeps killing mankind because the dominion mandate was truncated by man.

THE RESTORATION OF DOMINION TO MAN.

After man was sent out of Eden, the condition of man continue to grow worse that after a little while man started living like animals, killing each other, dominating and bullying each other to the point that all the intents of man's heart was certified by God to be evil all the time. In God's plan to redeem and restore man, he introduced laws that controlled how man should relate with God, man and other animals/creations of God. This became what was known as the law which God gave through Moses, the servant of God. This was not God's preferred solution to mankind, it was meant to manage the deteriorating condition of man until solution arrives.

"But when (In God's plan) the proper time had fully come, God sent his son, born of a woman, born under the (regulations of the) law, so that he might redeem& liberate those who were under the law, that we (who believe) might be adopted as sons (as God's children with all rights as fully grown members of a family)" Gal 4:4-5.

The Father has always been displeased with what had become of the man he made to rule the physical realm just as God himself is the ruler of all realms. But then, there was the plan of the redemption of man; in which God took the form of man and came to take the place of man and bore our sins and iniquity and was crucified on the cross. Jesus the saviour of the world came, not to satisfy the requirement of God's anger, but to fulfill the requirements of God's law that man may be brought back to God. By the suffering and death of Christ, man's iniquity was washed away and we became reconciled to God and the sin that always kept us away from God, the same sin that drove man out of the garden was taken away. However, something so amazing also happened, we became adopted sons of God, translated out of the realms of earth to seat with Christ in the heavenly realm from there to operate here on earth. There was a restoration to the order like in the beginning, to rule the earth from a realm above the earth.

One of the sweetest things about man's redemption is that we ascended to a realm far above Eden, because in Eden, God came down – at the cool of the evening because he didn't dwell there, but in Christ, we ascended to the kingdom of God's dear son – which is at the right hand side of God the Father, where we are seated together with the Lord.

In addition to that, a new mandate was given to us in Christ Jesus, it is far greater than the dominion mandate in Eden; its influence surpassed just the earth, but even other realms above the earth.

"Go ye into all the world and preach the gospel to every creature. He that believeth and is baptized shall be saved; but he that believeth not shall be damned. And these signs shall follow them that believe, in my name shall they cast out devils; they shall speak with new tongues; they shall take up serpents and if they drink any deadly thing, it shall not hurt them; they shall lay hands on the sick and they shall recover." Mark 16: 15 – 16

"Behold, I give unto power to tread on serpents and scorpions, and over all the powers of the enemy, and nothing shall by any means hurt you." Luke 10:19

In Christ Jesus we still have the dominion over the creatures of earth, the birds of the air, the fish of the sea, but much more than that is the dominion over Satan and his demons which was not there before.

Let's breakdown this dominion mandate in Christ for better understanding.

1. CAST OUT DEVILS

This is not a ministry in the body of Christ; it is a job/assignment for every believer. We have been given the mandate to cast out devils anywhere we find them on earth because they are intruders. Just same way the lord casted them out whenever he encountered them during him ministry on earth. As a child of God who has been translated to the heavenly, you have the authority in your words to cast out devils once you encounter them be it in your dream or in reality.

2. SPEAK WITH NEW TONGUES

This is just like it happened at Pentecost, we have been given mandate to speak in tongues and this is activated when the Holy Ghost fills you as a believers. Many people because they don't understand what the tongues are saying think it's worthless, but it is not.

In fact the power in speaking in tongues is limitless, so much that it can gather a whole city to hear you speak. If you need a city to hear at your voice, speak the tongues. When we pray in tongues, we speak mysteries.

"There are, it may be, so many kinds of sound in the world, and none is without meaning" 1 Cor. 14:10 (New Heart English bible)

Every word you speak by tongue have a meaning. When we speak in tongues we communicate with the Lord by the spirit and the Lord understands what we speak. Tongues is the only language that communicates both meanings & emotions in itself. As a new creature, we must learn to speak in tongues more often.

3. TAKE UP SERPENTS

This portion of our dominion mandate is literal to mean that as a child of God you can pick up snakes with your hands and it will not hurt you. The implication of this is the fact that in Eden there was an enmity between the serpent (literal snake representing the beast of earth) and man. In fact serpent was the only creature God openly declared to strike man, while man will crush its head. But here, that enmity is taken away such that the believer in Christ has a restored dominion over the beast of the earth like Daniel, we can be in a lion's den and will not be attacked.

However there is also a spiritual implication to this phrase. The serpent at Eden was a form the evil one (referring to Satan) took to deceive the woman. So when our dominion mandate declares we will take up serpent, it also implies that Satan cannot limit us anymore. We will take up serpents not as friends but a foe whose weapon of attack has been rendered powerless against us. So like the serpent, all his weapons, -venom and poisons (powers) have been rendered powerless when he tries to use it against a believer in Christ and he knows too. So the potency of Satan's power becomes impotent when he tries to exercise it on a believer in Christ Jesus.

4. IF THEY DRINK ANY DEADLY THING, IT SHALL NOT HURT THEM

This portion of our dominion mandate did not say when they pray and drink, rather if they didn't know or they know but cannot stop that from happening, if they drink poison it will not hurt them. So when evil men try to poison you a believer in Christ, the poison will lose its potency when you take it. Maybe it's a portion to make you behave in a particular manner, it is not meant to work in your system child of God. There is a power at work within us that will not allow such external power take over us. This is one of the reasons why the Holy Ghost lives within you. This is part of the dividends of being a vessel for the spirit of God. If you know this you will not be scared of evil man because you know they can do you no harm

5. LAY HANDS ON THE SICK& THEY SHALL RECOVER

This is not a ministry; this is the right of a believer in Christ Jesus. It does not require a special grace or anointing. It is given for all who are citizens of Christ Jesus. You have the mandate to heal the sick wherever you see them.

You do not have to be a healing evangelist, or figure out what will happen, all you need to do, as a believer in Christ Jesus, when you encounter sick people, lay hands on them and make them recover. The command is not to pray for sick people to recover, the scripture says to place your hands on the sick and they will recover. This is not because of fasting and prayer it is just because it is the mandate of heaven over you who have been translated to God's right hand of power. Many times God's word will not produce the result it declares when we try to add to it. The word of God the way God spoke it has the right ingredients to perform what God has promised but when we try to add to it, we either over salt it hence it falls short of the requirement to yield result. If you want to see the power of God in your life, apply God's word exactly the way it was given, don't change the design or coat it with anything.

The word of God is like silver & gold that have been tried 7 times in the fire hence it is pure; anything you add to it becomes dross to make it impure.

"The promises of the Lord can be trusted, and they are as genuine as silver refined seven times in the furnace". Ps 12: 16 Good News

The word of God is perfect in itself; the promises of God are complete requiring no support or additions to it. All that has been limiting us is that most times the word sound so simple that we disbelieve it. The requirements of God's word are so easy that we think it cannot perform what it has promised being that simple so we add things to it to make it complicated. The secret to manifesting God's power is to apply the word of God the same way it was written or spoken as the case may be. Anything else will hinder the power of God from flowing through his word.

God is an Artist or smith and he works with only pure gold or pure silver. The word of God spoken by the spirit of God or written by men of old is like pure Gold/ silver. If you want the Artist to make something beautiful for you, you must first being pure silver or gold.

"Take the impurities out of silver and the artist/ smith can produce a thing of beauty". Prov. 25:4 Good News

The word of God is a perfect Gold/ silver, just give it back to God the same way it was spoken or written. Do not try to add to it or remove from it, and God the smith man will make something beautiful out of his word for you to today. This applies to all the words of God's promise written in the scriptures not just the mandates in Christ Jesus that we are discussing, all other promises of God are same. No matter who is adding the dross, be it a bishop or pope, it can only limit the word of God. Remember what the smith requires is pure gold/ silver and that is exactly what God's word is.

In Christ Jesus, the most important commodity is not anointing or grace or any other thing men parrots about in this generation. The most important thing is the word of God. Once you find the word, careless about the anointing or grace because the word has in itself, all the ingredients to bring itself to pass, all you must do is to give it to the smith just as it was given you, undiluted, and unpolluted.

To give the word back to God simply means to apply the word as instructed. To do the bidding of that word you received without fail. No matter how foolish or childish or simple it could be, even if it sounds unreasonable in your estimation, just obey exactly as you were instructed, then you will see what the smith will make out of that word. When peter went to Joppa and there was a woman called Dorcas who was dead but because of her good deeds they would not bury her. When peter go to the scene he did not pray or sing but just did the exact thing the word (Jesus) always did when he raised the dead so he said "Tabitha get up" and that was it. The word of God is so powerful that it can perform just anything it says but when we begin to mix it with dross call it your "anointing" it loses power.

6. POWER TO TREAD ON SERPENTS AND SCORPIONS

According to theology, serpents and scorpions are not literal in this scripture, but refer to a most dreaded form of Satan's power. These two forms of Satan's power he uses to deceive the world and destroy men. Like serpent, he speaks seductive words to attract people while its venom is on its tail which it uses to strike and destroy the person (this is exactly what pornography is about, as a young person, it feels entertaining to watch pornography and on the surface it all about enjoyment and fun and how to explore God's gift of sex, but the venom in the tail is your mind being poisoned to think sex is about subjugation and molestation which is practically what pornography is about, gradually the demons get hold of your mind and every girl you see, you want to practice what you have being watching on her until you get in to trouble or destroy yourself).

But serpents and scorpion as forms of enemies' power all seek to take control of one place – your heart. When a serpent strikes or a scorpion, the venom only seek to reach one place – the heart to effect its action and take over the man. The same way Satan seeks to use the media to manipulate even the believer in Christ, but the promise of God, the mandate of the recreated man is that you will tread it under your feet,. It will not have a hold on you.

7. POWER OVER ALL THE POWERS OF THE ENEMY

The word "all" means everything. So we have authority to counter and subdue –all the powers of the enemy, no matter what the manifestation is and it shall not hurt us. So any way the enemy comes to manifest his powers, we in Christ Jesus have the authority to tread it under our feet and cancel it. Whether he manifest through a man or Satan himself, we have the mandate to handle him and put all his power to check.

This is the mandate of the recreated man in Christ Jesus. This is what Jesus bought for us by his blood. So therefore, there is no need to mourn over the Eden mandate that was lost when we have a better mandate in Christ Jesus.

In fact God himself is pleased when we exercise these mandates of the recreated man in Christ Jesus. It is yours and mine, let's walk in it. This is your place in Christ Jesus, a place of dominion, a place of authority and safety, a place of power at the right hand of the Father. This is Christ Jesus where we belong

Cheers

MIX
Papier aus verantwortungsvollen Quellen
Paper from responsible sources
FSC® C105338

Printed by Books on Demand GmbH, Norderstedt / Germany